The Complete and Easy Guide to

Social Security, Healthcare Rights, and Government Benefits

The Complete and Easy Guide to

Social Security, Healthcare Rights, and Government Benefits

by Faustin F. Jehle

A PUBLICATION OF
Emerson-Adams Press
Boca Raton, Florida 33486

Cataloging-in-Publication data available from Library of Congress.

Emerson-Adams Press
1259 South West 14th Street
Boca Raton, Florida 33486
(561) 391-0964
www.emerson-adamspress.com

International Standard Book Number 1-892-80314-3

First Printing, July 1998
10 9 8 7 6 5 4 3 2 1

Publisher's note: We have made a good faith effort to include accurate and up-to-date information. However, the publisher cannot guarantee the facts herein or the consequences of their use.

Dedication

Dedicated to my wife Rosemary,
whose love and patience
made this work possible.

Preface

Throughout my career as legal counsel to a major New York publisher, I found myself answering the same questions over and over again. And those questions had a familiar theme: benefits. Eventually I wrote a successful book, that sold nearly a million copies, about healthcare rights and benefits that put all the information people needed in an easy-to-use format.

Now, I have written a new book on Social Security, healthcare rights and government benefits such as Medicare, Medicaid, Disability, Supplemental Security Income (SSI), HMOs and managed care. This is an up-to-date, comprehensive guide that will answer the questions that worry us all: Am I covered? Do I need Medigap insurance? What will my Social Security benefits be when I retire? Will Social Security even be there when I retire? What do I do if my HMO turns me down for a procedure my doctor says I need?

It is my fervent hope that anyone who has concerns about these issues can turn to these pages and find the answers he or she needs. Whether a senior citizen or a single mom ... a two-career professional couple or a newly arrived immigrant ... this book seeks to simplify the government and insurance jargon and double-speak and clearly and completely explain your rights and benefits.

I find it very satisfying to provide people with such a useful and necessary resource.

Faustin J. Jehle
West Palm Beach, Florida

About the Author

Faustin J. Jehle is a the former legal counsel for a major New York publisher. After distinguished military service, Mr. Jehle received his BS, BBA, LLB, and JSD from St. John's University in New York. After a successful legal career, he turned some of his attention to writing a book on Social Security and Medicare—a book that went on to sell over 900,000 copies in 13 editions. His latest book, published by Emerson-Adams Press, is again a dedicated effort to provide people with easy-to-understand information on the rights and benefits that concern them most.

Publisher's Statement

We are proud to have been selected as the publisher of this timely and useful book by Faustin Jehle. To serve as the publisher of this unique, important, and helpful book is an honor. To work with Faustin Jehle, a well-respected, diligent, and thoughtful author is a true pleasure.

Others have been most helpful in the development and publication of this book. In particular, Erica Orloff for her thoughtful, careful, and creative editing, and overall supervision of the publishing process. The typesetting and page design was professionally done by Mark Manofsky, and the attractive new cover design and art work was created by Jonathan Pennell.

Also very important was the valuable assistance and meaningful input provided by several reviewers of the manuscript during the development process. In particular, David Machanic in Charlotte, Vermont, was very thoughtful, precise, and helpful with his suggestions for improvement. Professor Ronald Blum in Timonium, Maryland, provided detailed and valuable suggestions; Professor Arthur Rubens from the Division of Public Administration at Florida Gulf Coast University in Fort Myers, Florida, was very positive in providing his thoughtful suggestions for improvement in the overall organization and coverage of the book. I am personally indebted to each of these individuals for their thought, energy, and efforts.

Special acknowledgment must be given to our longtime friend, Professor Jeanne Barry Madigan, of Incline Village, Nevada, for her efforts in providing a detailed scientific analysis of the verbal complexity of the manuscript. Professor Barry's analysis served as a guide towards modifying the reading level which assisted in the use of more clear easy-to-read English language. Her professional input helped greatly towards simplifying the reading level of many of the related complex rules and regulations.

In addition, I want to acknowledge and offer many thanks to my wife, Martha R. Murphy, for her uncomplaining involvement with her secretarial/administrative efforts. Very important for me is to say thank you to the author's wife, Rosemary, for her behind-the-scenes support and encouragement and for so pleasantly handling the frequent telephone calls, fax, and correspondence.

This is a wonderful group of highly intelligent, thoughtful, concerned individuals whose combined efforts have contributed to the creation and publication of this significant and useful book. The coverage in this book will hopefully provide guidance to a wide array of readers in need of assistance in coping with these complex programs, while providing meaningful current information leading to workable solutions to perplexing, often difficult, problems.

My sincere hope is that you, the readers, will find this book helpful and your life made more pleasant by having this book available for your use and benefit.

Frederick H. Murphy
Publisher

Subject

Table of Contents

Introduction

What will my Social Security benefits be when I retire? Can I take early retirement? Do I need supplemental health insurance for my Medicare? Does Medicare cover the procedure I need? Am I covered? What if I am disabled? A veteran? These are questions that need straight answers. Unfortunately, if you have ever tried to decipher a government document, you know that straight answers are hard to find.

In addition, the history of the American Social Security program includes many changes. In fact, laws change constantly and changes were added to this book right up to publication. How does the average American stay informed? How can anyone wade through the mountains of government documents and extract the information that is really valuable?

This book began as a response to the countless questions about Social Security, HMOs, managed care, disability payments, Family Leave Act and other government-guaranteed rights and benefits. People need complete and easy answers and this book tries to provide them. It aims to be thorough and straightforward and is written by one of the country's foremost experts on these rights and benefits.

This book will be helpful to anyone seeking information on:

Social Security
Medicare
Medicaid
HMOs
Family Leave Act
Patient's Rights
Supplemental Security Income
Disability
Veteran's Rights
Medigap Insurance
Immigrants' Rights
Food Stamps

It includes valuable resources, such as addresses and information on:

Vital Statistics Offices for all 50 states
Social Security's Toll-Free number
National Archives
Where to report Medicare fraud and abuse
State Medicaid Offices for all 50 states

It also includes a sample living will and durable power of attorney for healthcare, as well as a comprehensive index so that the reader can quickly find any information needed. It answers questions senior citizens ask as well as those questions confronting young families. This is a book for everyone.

In short, this is a comprehensive and complete resource on the issues that worry all Americans. Used as a guide, it can take away some of the anxiety and confusion swirling around these issues. You may wish to read this book cover to cover to get a sense of the scope of various benefits. But most likely, this will become a useful aid to turn to on specific questions. May you read on and find the answers you have been seeking.

CHAPTER ONE
Social Security

HISTORY

This program, known as the Old Age Survivors and Disability Insurance (OASDI), was signed into law in 1935. Over the years, this act (SSA) has been amended many times to meet the healthcare and financial needs of all Americans.

In 1940, survivors benefits were added and then disability benefits in 1956. The Medicare program for the elderly and disabled and Medicaid, the public assistance program for low-income people, including families with children, the aged, blind and disabled, were enacted and became effective in 1965. Supplemental Security Income (SSI) for low-income, blind and disabled persons replaced several prior programs and was enacted and became part of the Social Security Act in 1972.

The main purpose of these social insurance programs was to provide widespread protection for all Americans against risks to which we are all subject, including loss of income in old age.

With all of the changes we have experienced to date, it is easy to understand that the costs of such programs will grow with the coverage provided and the increase in the numbers of persons receiving benefits. Social Security and Medicare benefits are an earned right. Eligibility is established by work in covered employment and by payroll tax contributions. Workers pay taxes under the Federal Insurance Contributions Act (FICA) or under the Self-Employment Contributions Act (SECA) and earn credits, referred to as *quarters of coverage*. The number of credits earned on a job or in self-employment establishes the insurance status of the individual. Such status can be "fully insured" or "currently insured" and establishes the worker's eligibility for various benefits.

SOCIAL SECURITY CREDITS

Eligibility for Social Security benefits is based on whether you have earned enough credits on a job or in self-employment or a combination of both and have paid the FICA or SECA payroll taxes on earnings. This is referred to by the SSA as "covered employment."

A quarter of coverage or credit is earned for any three-month period of a year, beginning with January, in which a worker or self-employed person received $780 or more in earnings for covered employment.

In 2000, you receive a credit for each $780 earned upon which you pay taxes, but you cannot earn more than four credits for any year regardless of the amount of money you earn. For example, if you earned $3,120 in a single month, four credits would be earned, i.e., on $2,960 ($740 times four).

The fact that you only earn four QCs per year does not have anything to do with the dollar amount of benefits you or your family will receive. What you earn above this amount, up to the maximum earnings subject to FICA or SECA taxes, will increase your benefit.

The Social Security Administration keeps a record of your year-to-year "covered earnings" and can provide you with an estimate of the Social Security benefit you would be entitled to receive at 65, or at 62, if you

For those who have been working for many years and wish to compute the number of credits they may have earned over the years, the following table shows the earnings amount required in prior years to earn one (1) credit of coverage or quarter of coverage (QC):

QCs by Year					
1978	$250	1986	$440	1994	$620
1979	$260	1987	$460	1995	$630
1980	$290	1988	$470	1996	$640
1981	$310	1989	$500	1997	$650
1982	$340	1990	$520	1998	$700
1983	$370	1991	$540	1999	$740
1984	$390	1992	$570	2000	$780
1985	$410	1993	$590		

decide to take benefits at that earlier age. You can request a mailing of your statement, if needed. You can obtain a Personal Earnings and Benefit Estimate Statement (PEBES) from your local Social Security office. If you are now 60 or older, you may have already received this statement. After 1999, automatic mailings of PEBES will be made to all persons over 25 years of age. You can request a form by calling 1-800-772-1213.

The local SSA office is open weekdays during regular business hours, usually 9 A.M. to 5 P.M. The SSA Toll Free number 1-800-772-1213 is available weekdays from 7 A.M. to 7 P.M. The recording you will hear provides a number of options for information. You may leave a message and ask for a SSA representative to return your call if the line is busy or a representative is not currently available. To avoid delays on the line, call early in the morning or late afternoon Wednesday through Friday.

If your problem is a complex one or if an interpreter is required, the local office of SSA is suggested rather than the toll-free call to obtain information.

The SSA is required by law to provide translators or interpreters for non-English-speaking persons and to make home visits for housebound individuals who are unable to conduct their business by telephone or mail. The SSA publishes information pamphlets in many languages which may be obtained from the local office or by calling the SSA at 410-965-7863. Some local offices have interpreters and translators, but if the language is unusual to the area, an interpreter may not be available, and you may have to bring your own.

For those who have a computer, access to SSA information over the Internet will provide a great amount of data. The Internet address for electronic mail document service is: info@ssa.gov; with Mosaic, www.ssa.gov; with Gopher, Gopher.ssa.gov.

SOCIAL SECURITY ELIGIBILITY AND BENEFIT AMOUNTS

The amount of retirement benefits—the amount you or your spouse or dependents receive—depends on how much you have earned under covered employment and your age when you elect to begin drawing benefits. The basic benefit amount from which all benefits on your record are derived is computed from your earnings record by calculating what the SSA calls the Average Indexed Monthly Earnings (AIME) and from that, the Primary Insurance Amount (PIA).

Your PEBES will tell you in detail, based on your earnings, what your current status is:

- How many credits you have.
- The estimated benefit amounts for your retirement at ages 62, 65, and after 70.
- The figure used for your Primary Insurance Amount (shown as the estimated benefit amount at age 65).
- Your estimated survivors' and disability benefits.

All the estimates on your PEBES are based on the earnings the SSA has on record for you from your first covered employment through approximately 12 months before your request, plus what you told them you expect to earn between the time of the request and the time you plan to begin benefits. The closer you are to being ready to begin collecting benefits, the nearer the estimates will be to the actual figure you will receive. A request for a PEBES is not an application for benefits. To receive any benefit, you must apply for it.

Entitlement and Benefits: Retired Worker

If you are a fully insured worker, you are now entitled to collect retirement benefits beginning as early as the first full month in which you are age 62. The amount of your benefit depends on when, between that time and reaching age 70, you elect to begin receiving benefits.

In 2000, those first accepting benefits at age 62 receive a permanently reduced benefit equal to 80% of a full benefit; those who turn age 62 in 1998 but wait until they turn age 70 in the year 2005 will receive a permanently increased benefit equal to 127.5% of a full benefit.

Today, the earliest you can receive your full unreduced benefit (100% of your PIA) is age 65 (unless you are disabled). Your PEBES gives you this figure as an estimate based on the figures you provided and adjusted for anticipated national average wage growth.

Early retirement permanently reduces the basic benefit for each month from the time you begin collecting benefits. If you have taken early retirement benefits and die before your spouse, the widow or widower's benefit will be reduced. Delaying retirement past NRA will permanently increase the benefits paid to you and ultimately to your surviving spouse (and possibly divorced spouse), as well as any other benefits paid on your PMI.

Entitlement and Benefits: Spouse (Husband and Wife)

If you are a fully insured worker, a spousal benefit of 50% (or less) of your basic benefit can be paid on your work record to:

- Your husband or wife at age 62 or older.
- Your husband or wife under age 62, if he or she is taking care of your child (in some cases, dependent grandchild) who is under age 16 or a child of any age who became disabled before age 22.
- Your former wife or husband age 62 or older if you were married at least 10 years.

Up to 100% of your basic benefit can be paid to your widower or widow (or divorced spouse) as a survivors' benefit. The payment for a divorced spouse is 50% of the worker's basic benefit (PIA) if the worker retired at age 65 and the spouse first accepts benefits at 65 or older. If the worker retires earlier than age 65, the percentage for the spouse's benefit remains the same, but because the benefit amount from which it is calculated is less, the check will be less.

To put it another way, the spouse's benefit is paid as an auxiliary benefit, so it is reduced if the base it's being paid on has been reduced. If the spouse also chooses to retire before the normal retirement age, it is reduced further—currently, 25/36 of 1% for each month of entitlement before 65.

A spouse's benefit is not reduced for age if he or she is caring for an entitled child of the worker, but that benefit is subject to a family maximum.

Divorced Spouse (Husband or Wife)

A divorced spouse is entitled to benefits on a former husband's or wife's work record if the marriage lasted at least ten years. The divorced spouse must be at least 62 and unmarried, and the worker must be 62 or older.

If the former husband and wife have been divorced at least two years, the divorced spouse is entitled to benefits even if the insured worker has not yet retired. If the worker was receiving benefits before the divorce, the two-year rule does not apply.

The benefit payment to a qualified divorced spouse is the same as for a spouse. If the worker on whose record these benefits are based has remarried, the family maximums do not include the divorced spouse.

Dependent Child and Grandchild

Social Security defines a dependent child as one under the age of 18 (or 19 if still in high school full-time) or one with a continuing disability that began before the age of 22. Such a child (grandchild, great-grandchild, a natural child, stepchild, or a child adopted or born out of wedlock) is entitled to benefits on an insured worker's work record.

If a grandchild's or great-grandchild's natural or adoptive parents are deceased or were disabled when the grandparents became entitled to retirement or to disability benefits, or when those grandparents died, each dependent child is entitled to benefits if the grandparents or great-grandparents provided his or her support.

The payment to a child of a retired or disabled worker is 50% of the retired worker's benefit for each child, subject to the family maximum.

The payment to a child of a worker who has died is 75% of that worker's benefit, subject to the family maximum.

If both parents are deceased, a child qualifies for benefits on the work record of either parent, whichever yields the higher benefit. If the child marries, the benefits stop.

The benefit amount for each entitled dependent grandchild is the same: 50% of the grandparent worker's benefit if the grandparent is living and 75% if the grandparent is deceased, subject to the family maximum. These rules apply for great-grandchildren as well.

A child's earnings can affect his or her benefits, as they are subject to the exempt earnings rule.

Many young people feel that Social Security taxes that are paid by their parents or by them is an unnecessary burden upon the family and that such monies could be more efficiently spent on other bills or saved for their education.

However, when unexpected illness, injury or death of a parent occurs, points of view change and give new meaning to the importance of Social Security to every member of the family. For some, Social Security benefits to the family could be as high as $2,000 per month.

In 1999, more than 3.8 million children were receiving benefits amounting to $1.4 billion. These benefits were paid to natural born, adopted, step-children and dependent grandchildren of qualified workers.

Children entitled to benefits:

1. Those who have a parent who is disabled, or retired and entitled to receive Social Security benefits; or
2. Whose parent was "fully insured" or "currently insured" under Social Security at the time of death; and
3. The child is under 18 or between 18 and 19 and a full-time student.

The worker's PIA is determined by the covered wages earned by the worker and the amount of time worked over the years. The worker's PIA is available from the local Social Security office, or by calling the Social Security Administration Hotline (1-800-772-1213) or by filing a personal earnings and benefit estimate statement (PEBES) Form SSA 7004 PC-opi.

There is, however, a limit on the amount of Social Security benefits that will be paid to a family. It is referred to as the maximum family benefit (MFB) and is determined when the benefit is computed. Generally the MFB is 150% to 180% of the worker's primary insurance amount (PIA).

If the total benefit payable to the family, including the child or children, exceed the MFB, then the benefit payable to each member of the family will be reduced proportionately (except that the worker's benefit is not reduced) until the total benefit being paid to the family equals the MFB allowable amount.

While a qualified divorced spouse of a covered worker may receive benefits, the benefits paid to such spouse are not counted in computing MFB and are not reduced.

Survivors' Benefits (Widow or Widower)

A surviving spouse age 60 or over is entitled to payment if the worker is fully or currently insured at the time of death.

Regardless of age, a widow or widower (or divorced widow or widower) who is caring for an entitled child of the deceased worker gets benefits if the worker was either fully or currently insured and the child is under 16 or disabled. This benefit also applies to a surviving divorced spouse meeting the same conditions, or if the divorced widow or widower is disabled.

The amounts of survivors' benefits vary, depending both on how much the deceased worker was entitled to and what category the survivor or survivors fall into. Currently, the payment to a widow or widower at age 65 is 100% of the worker's benefit if, at the time of the worker's death, the worker was receiving (or could have received) full benefits. If the worker was receiving reduced benefits before he or she died, the same reduced benefit would go to the surviving spouse. Permanent increases, i.e., benefits that result from delaying retirement past age 65 are also passed along to the widow/widower. If the surviving spouse elects to take the benefit before she or he reaches 65, the amount is reduced by 0.475% (19/40 of 1%) of the benefit amount for each month of entitlement before age 65.

Example

If you apply at 60, there are 60 months (12 × 5 years) to reduce. Multiply 60 × 0.475 to get the total percent of reduction. It comes to 28.5%, so the payment would be 71.5% of the benefit.

A widow or widower caring for an entitled child or children under 16 or disabled is also eligible for 75% of the worker's benefit as a parent's benefit.

These benefits are all subject to the *maximum family benefit* allowed.

Disabled Widow or Widower

Under certain circumstances a benefit equal to 71.5% of the deceased worker's PIA can be paid to a disabled surviving spouse, aged 50 to 59.

Divorced Widow or Widower

The rules that apply to surviving spouses also apply to divorced surviving spouses, provided the marriage lasted for 10 years before the divorce and the survivor is not married at the time of applying for benefits.

If more than one divorced spouse, or a divorced spouse and the spouse married to the worker at the time of his or her death, both apply for survivors' benefits on the same worker's record, the benefits paid to a divorced spouse are paid independently of the family maximum and do not affect the benefits paid to other survivors.

Dependent Parents of a Worker Who Dies

Dependent parents (or only one parent), age 62 or over, are eligible for benefits if the worker was fully insured at the time of death. To qualify, dependent parents must show that the worker was providing at least one-half of their support.

To show this, a statement must be prepared listing the amounts paid out over the period of support for food, clothing, shelter, and medical and dental care. Attach canceled checks, receipts, or charge account bills to demonstrate that the worker contributed more than 50% of the cost of these items, and submit them through your local Social Security office.

The payment to one parent is 82.5% of the deceased worker's benefit. If both parents are alive and eligible, the benefit amount is 150% of the basic benefit, adjusted for the family maximum.

TIMING YOUR RETIREMENT

If you have some choice about when to stop working as well as when to start taking benefits, be sure you examine all the options carefully and be aware of the time limitations you have in which to make changes in your status. For example, when you are near retirement from your job, if you can choose the time when you will stop working, remember that you can work until you earn the maximum allowable under that year's earnings limitation, then retire and not lose any of that year's benefits.

In determining when to file for your retirement benefits and under which record to file—should you have that option—the best guidance is to be found in your Personal Earnings and Benefit Estimate Statement. It will give you the information you need to evaluate the effect your individual options have on your particular benefits. Remember, the nearer you are to applying for benefits, the more accurate and more useful to you the estimates in your PEBES will be.

UNDERSTANDING REDUCTION OF RETIREMENT BENEFITS

The Social Security law reduces your benefits if you elect to receive your benefits before normal retirement age (NRA) of 65.

To avoid confusion as to how such reductions may affect the decision of the worker, the worker's spouse, or the widow(er) of such worker the following explanation is offered.

1. Assume that the worker's primary insurance amount (PIA) on which benefits are computed is $1,000. If the worker elects to receive benefits at 65, the benefit would be $1,000.

2. If the worker decides to receive the retirement benefit at 62, that $1,000 will be reduced by five-ninths of 1% (1/180) for each month that the worker is under 65 when the benefits start. In this case at 62, 36 months times 1/180 times $1,000 or a reduction of $200 (rounded up to $200, from $199.99).

3. Normally the spouse of such worker is entitled to 50% of the worker's PIA or $500 at 65. However if the spouse elects to receive such benefit before 65, that $500 is reduced by 25/36 (1/144) for each of the months that the spouse is under 65 when benefits commence. If the benefits are taken at 63, the reduction would be $500 times 24 times 1/144 or $83.33 rounded to $83.40. The benefit would be $416.60.

4. A widow(er) of the covered worker can receive benefits at 60, or can wait until 65—the NRA. At 65, the benefit would be 100% of the worker's PIA or $1,000. If the widow(er) elects to receive benefits after 60 but before 65, that benefit would be reduced by 19/40 of 1% (19/4000) for each month that the widow(er) is under 65 when the benefit commences. If election is made at 62 the reduction would be $1000 times 36 times 19/4000 or a reduction of $171. The benefit would be $1,000 less $171 or $829.

5. If the worker elected to receive benefits before 65, the widow(er)'s benefit cannot exceed the deceased worker's reduced benefit or 82.5% of the deceased worker's PIA whichever is the largest amount.

6. The disabled widow(er) who may elect to receive benefits before age 60 would be entitled to 71.5% of the deceased worker's PIA.

Retiring at the Normal Retirement Age

At present, full retirement benefits under Social Security begin at age 65; this is the age

Benefits as a Percentage of Covered Worker's PIA at Specific Ages

Retirement Benefits for	Age	%PIA
Covered Worker		
At normal retirement	65	100.0
Before normal retirement	64	93.3
	63	86.6
	62	80.0
Disability	any age	100.0
Blindness	55 or over	100.0
Spouse of Retired or Disabled Worker		
At spouse's normal retirement age	65	50.0
	64	45.8
	63	41.7
	62	37.5
Child of Deceased Worker		75.0
Child of Retired or Disabled Worker		50.0
Widow(er) or Divorced Widow(er) of Worker		
At widow(er)'s normal retirement age	65	100.0
	63	88.6
	60	71.5
Disabled Widow(er) or Disabled Divorced Widow(er)	50–60	71.5
Widow(er) (Mother or Father) Caring for Child Under 16 or Disabled		75.0
Dependent Parent of Deceased Worker		
One Parent	62	82.0
Two parents (payable to each parent)	62	75.0

Note: Benefits for families are subject to the "Maximum Family Benefit."

which the SSA considers to be the normal retirement age (NRA).

The NRA is going to increase gradually during the next two decades until it reaches age 67. As the increases in the NRA begin for people reaching age 62 in 2000, those who were born in 1938 or later will be the ones affected. The age increase applies to Social Security only; it does not change the age of eligibility for Medicare.

The increase in the NRA will not change the availability of reduced benefits at 62 (or 60 for widows and widowers). But it does, over time, increase the amount the benefit will be reduced, from up to 20% to up to 30% (remaining at 20% for widows and widowers). Again, these changes will be gradual and will apply only to those reaching age 62 in 2000 and thereafter.

"Retired" doesn't mean not working. The SSA uses the term to mean you have begun collecting Social Security retirement benefits.

Choosing Early Retirement

The longer you wait between ages 62 and 65 to begin receiving benefits, the smaller the reduction in your PIA will be, as the table on page 7 shows.

Your basic benefit or primary insurance amount (PIA) will be reduced by 0.555%, or 5/9 of 1%, for each month in which you take your benefit before you become 65.

Example
James begins collecting benefits at age 63, 24 months before entitlement at age 65. Multiply 24 × 0.555 to get the total percent of reduction; it rounds off to 13.33%. So in this case, his benefit is reduced by 13.33%. The benefit check would be 86.67% of his basic benefit or PIA.

To receive benefits for the month you become 62, you must be 62 for all days of that month. Once again, if you choose to collect Social Security earlier than age 65, your benefit is permanently reduced (disregarding

the annual cost-of-living adjustment) and it will not increase to your full PIA at age 65.

Retiring, Then Changing Your Mind and Going Back to Work Again

You can change your mind about working even if you have already begun collecting benefits. Benefits will continue to be paid. When you go back to work, you must inform the SSA. This is done by submitting an Annual Report of Earnings form, which you can order by telephone or get from your local SSA office.

If you have told the Social Security Administration that you won't be earning over the limit for the year, but you do, you still receive the benefits. The SSA will simply collect any amount it overpaid by deducting the overpayment from future benefits. You must report your annual earnings to SSA by April 15 of the following year.

Choosing to Work While Collecting Benefits

Earning money while collecting Social Security is a necessity for some, an option for others. Some people continue working just as they always have, past 62 (or 65), and elect to begin receiving their benefits at the same time.

If you have a choice, be aware that it isn't a simple matter of adding your earnings to the amount the government sends you—this can be quite a complicated decision. Working can have an effect on the amount of your benefit (it may raise or lower it) and there are other points to consider. Here are three critical things to think about:

■ Taxes: Earnings, whether from an employer or self-employment, are subject to federal income tax, Social Security, and Medicare payroll taxes (FICA and SECA), and, if applicable, to state and local income taxes. Social Security benefits may also be taxed

■ Exempt Earnings: Before age 70, there is a maximum amount you can earn in a year depending on your age without reducing your benefit. For 2000, if you are age 62 through age 64, the SSA reduces your benefit $1 for every $2 earned above $10,080. From age 65 through age 69, each $3 earned above $17,000 reduces your benefit by $1, however, see page 20.

However, if you (as a retired worker or beneficiary) do work, earn more than the exempt earnings, and therefore receive reduced benefit, you will still have more combined income benefits and earnings than if you had limited your earnings to the maximum amount.

After age 70, the maximum earnings rule no longer applies; all earnings are exempt. You still pay taxes, but no matter what you earn, your benefit is not reduced.

■ Recomputation: Another consideration is the possibility of an increased primary benefit through recomputation because of higher earnings. If you have annual earnings in any year between ages 65 and 70 that are as high or higher than your highest pre-age 65 earnings, these earnings might raise your average earnings enough to result in a higher PIA.

Again, increasing your basic benefit through higher earnings after age 65 will also raise the benefit paid to anyone else who receives payments based on your work record.

Filing for Benefits Later than Age 65

The surest way to increase your primary benefit is by delaying your application for Social Security. The SSA will increase your benefit by a percentage that goes up with each year you delay retirement up to age 70. If you were born in 1924 or before, the rate is 3% a year for each year you wait. For people born in 1925 or 1926, the rate is 3.5%; for those born after 1926, the rate goes up another .5% each 2 years until it reaches 8%.

Unlike the increase in a benefit made by an increase in average earnings, the increase made by delayed retirement applies only to

the benefit paid to the worker or that worker's surviving spouse or ex-spouse.

BENEFITS FOR PEOPLE WITH DISABILITIES WHO WORK

Special rules make it possible for people with disabilities receiving Social Security or Supplemental Security Income (SSI) to work and still receive monthly benefits. These work incentive rules are slightly different from those for Social Security and SSI retired beneficiaries, but the goal for both is similar—to encourage people who want to work and to continue their benefits until they can work on a regular basis.

Disabled Social Security recipients can work for a nine-month trial period without having their earnings affect their Social Security benefits. Impairment-related work expenses may also be deducted when counting earnings. Chapters 2 and 5 provide more information on Disability Benefits and SSI.

If you are disabled, eligible for Social Security disability benefits or SSI, and wish to continue work, begin working, or train for a job, ask to discuss your special situation with your local Social Security work incentives expert.

FILING ON THE WORK RECORD OF A SPOUSE

Everyone has the choice as to when to begin collecting benefits; some people can also choose whether to file for benefits on their own work record or that of a husband or wife. You have to have been married at least one year (or less in some cases). Even if your spouse is deceased or you have been divorced and your former spouse has remarried, you may be entitled to file on his or her work record and may receive higher benefits if you do. In any case, you need to be aware of all your options.

As a husband or wife, you may receive benefits at any age if you're caring for the child (possibly grandchild) of a qualified retired, disabled, or deceased worker if that child is under age 16 or disabled before age 22. If you have no children or they are grown, you'll be eligible for half of your spouse's benefit when you reach age 65 or for a reduced benefit at age 62.

As a widow or widower, you may receive a survivors' benefit at any age if you're caring for a child who is under age 16 or disabled before age 22. Otherwise, you may receive benefits as early as age 60 or, if you are disabled, at age 50. Survivors' benefits range from 71.5% of a deceased worker's benefit amount (if they begin at age 60) to 100% (if you wait until age 65).

As a divorced spouse, you're entitled to the same benefits you would have received as a spouse or widowed spouse if your marriage lasted 10 years or more. (Length-of-marriage rules do not apply to survivors with minor children.) You may lose your right to these benefits if you remarry.

For the purpose of exploring the options available to people eligible to collect retirement benefits under more than one work record, let's look (at right column) at a situation where a person has these choices to make.

Two things to keep in mind when filing for Social Security—**you may be eligible for benefits under more than one work record, and you are always entitled to the highest benefit available**. When you make your application to the SSA, be sure to give them information on all the various work records under which you may be entitled to benefits. They will check your claim and pay you the highest benefit.

Different Kinds of Spouses

Besides being a divorced or widowed spouse, there is another circumstance under which someone might qualify for spousal benefits. This is a case in which a person has gone through a marriage ceremony which he or she believed to be legal but later found was not. Such a person, as of 1992, may be what is called a "deemed spouse." As such, he or she is eligible for the same benefits as a legal spouse.

Example

Suppose Rose, who divorced Harry after 15 years of marriage, has worked at covered employment off and on for 30 years and is a fully covered wage earner entitled to benefits on her own work record. She then marries Bill who is also a fully insured worker. They divorce 11 years later, and then Bill dies. Now, at 65 years of age, Rose wants to retire. Whose record should she use when she files for benefits?

For the sake of comparison, let's look at the 3 categories that cover Rose's situation: wage earner, unmarried divorced spouse, and widow. Rose is eligible for benefits as any one of the 3, since she was married to each of the men for more than 10 years.

Rose has earned more than enough work credits to qualify on her own work record. She has, however, worked at low-paying jobs, so her average earnings figure is not high, and her PIA is only going to be $460.

Harry, her first husband, is still alive and still working at age 70. He has always earned a good salary. Rose, as his eligible divorced spouse, is entitled to half his PIA of $1,270, which would give her $635. But the survivors' benefit as a divorced widow is all of Bill's PIA, or $1,150, so this is clearly the best choice.

Even though Rose is entitled to benefits under 3 categories, she can't collect them all. Instead, she is allowed to choose the highest-paying category, or whatever combination of benefits yields her the highest payment.

Suppose Rose is only 60 when she needs to begin collecting benefits. At that age, the only category under which she can file is as Bill's divorced widow. She's too young to get benefits as either a worker or divorced spouse of a worker.

For people who live together without being formally married, the situation may be different. Few states recognize common law marriages, and the Social Security Administration usually makes no provision for them when the state does not. If this is your situation, you need to determine what your state provides for in such cases. Being considered legally married can work either for you or against you. Although you cannot collect benefits as a spouse, if you are collecting 100% of a benefit as a widow or widower, you will not lose those benefits by living with someone without being legally married.

Lump-Sum Death Benefit

Regardless of a widow or widower's age, if the worker was either fully or currently insured at the time of death, a one-time payment of $255 is payable to the eligible surviving spouse.

Children of the worker may receive this benefit only if they are eligible for a benefit on the worker's income if there is no surviving spouse.

Though intended to pay for burial expenses, the benefit cannot be paid directly to a funeral home though it can be paid to someone other than the surviving spouse who has already paid the funeral bill. The Lump Sum Benefit is $255.

A claim for a lump sum death benefit must be filed with the Social Security office within 2 years of the worker's death.

THE "NOTCH"

"Notch" is the term used to refer to the difference in benefit amounts paid on similar earnings records to people who, because of when they were born, have had their benefits calculated under different formulas. What happens is that people born before 1917 received a windfall if they continued to work after age 62.

When automatic Cost-of-Living increases were enacted and factored into the formula in 1972, an error was introduced with them in the way inflation was calculated. This error caused people born from 1910 through 1916 to receive benefits that were greater than intended and would have eventually led to the bankruptcy of the system.

In 1977, Congress corrected the error by adopting the new benefit formula which applies to everyone born after 1921. That law, to ease the transition for those closest to retirement, provided that people born from 1917 through 1921 could use either the new formula or a special transition formula created for them to calculate their benefits. They could then take the higher of the two benefits.

The Senate asked the National Academy of Social Insurance to study the situation. The panel concluded that while the notch is unfortunate, a change would cost $50 to $300 billion dollars and no further change should be made.

The American Association of Retired Persons (AARP), though militant in protecting COLA's and fighting increases in Medicare premiums and taxes on benefits, also opposes efforts to change the notch. Their position is that the current benefit formula keeps the ratio of workers' benefits to earning history stable and fair.

If you would like to go into this question in more detail, the report of the National Academy of Social Insurance is available as SSA Publication 05-10042, which can be ordered from the Government Printing Office in Washington, D.C.

STUDENTS AGE 18 AND OVER

The benefits paid to a child of a retired, disabled, or deceased worker are terminated when the child reaches age 18. Benefits will be paid up to age 19 if the child is a full-time student at an elementary or secondary school in the month he or she reaches the age of 19. The child will remain eligible for benefits only for the semester or quarter during which he or she reaches age 19. If the school does not use the quarter or semester system, the student may be allowed to receive benefits for up to four months to complete the course.

Benefits for a child will also stop if the child marries, and children's benefits are subject to the exempt earnings rule and benefit checks are reduced by $1 for each $2 earned by the child above the 1998 ceiling of $9,120.

A disabled child of a retired or disabled worker may receive benefits (50% of the worker's PIA) after age 18 if the child's disability began before age 22. The benefits for a disabled child are also subject to the same exempt earnings rule as are those of a disabled wage earner. Benefits are usually terminated if the child marries. However, marriage to another childhood disability beneficiary will not terminate the benefit as long as both partners are at least age 18.

VETERANS

If you worked irregularly or very little after leaving military service, either because of illness or because of a lack of technical skills, the information below may be important to you, your spouse, and your children. If, on the other hand, you went to work after leaving military service and paid Social Security taxes on the maximum or near-maximum earnings, the information below may not apply to your benefit situation.

Entitlement to Credits

Since 1957, serving in the armed forces has been considered covered employment by Social Security, and FICA taxes have been withheld from military pay. If you were in active military service between 1940 and 1956, you are also entitled to 1 quarter (1 credit) of Social Security coverage for each of the calendar quarters you were in active service, provided you did not receive a dishonorable discharge.

For each month you were in active service, $160 of earnings is credited, even though no Social Security taxes were paid during the period 1940 to 1956. These wage credits are not payable as a separate benefit; rather, they are used, if needed, to establish insured status or to increase your benefit. You must file for benefits before a determination can be made as to whether or not these credits can be applied.

Proof Requirements

In order to claim your credits, you must furnish proof of your age, the time of your active service, and your record of service during that period. The Appendix explains how to request a certified copy of your military record.

Restrictions on Work Credits

Should you get credit toward military retirement benefits for military service in any of the armed forces, the SSA will not give you any work credits toward Social Security benefits covering the same time period, with the following exceptions:

- *Armed Forces Disability Benefits:* If you are receiving military retirement pay from the armed forces because of disability—rather than length of service—you are also entitled to credits for Social Security benefits covering the same time period. This is very important if you are a veteran of Korea or Vietnam, for you may be entitled to Social Security disability benefits *in addition* to your armed forces disability retirement benefits.

- *Length-of-Service-Retirees:* If you are a Length-of-Service retiree from the armed forces and were on active duty after 1950, you can receive credits for Social Security for each quarter during those periods—unless another federal agency is also using this same period of time to compute an annuity.

- *Widows and Widowers:* Under some circumstances, surviving spouses are permitted to waive the right to a civil service survivors' annuity and receive credit (not otherwise possible) for military service prior to 1957 to determine eligibility for, and the amount of, Social Security survivors' benefits.

SOCIAL SECURITY CREDITS (QCS)

Benefits under the Social Security Program are based on whether or not you have earned enough credits or quarters of coverage (QCs) either as an employee or in self-employment and have paid the Federal Insurance Contributions Act (FICA) or Self-employment Contributions Act (SECA) payroll taxes on such earnings. This status is referred to as "covered employment." All work is now covered by Social Security except for some but not all federal, state and local employees and a few religious orders which object to coverage.

The amount of earnings necessary for a credit or quarter of coverage for 2000 is $780. Self-employed workers need the same amount of income to earn a credit as wage earners.

Regardless of amount of earnings that you may have in any calendar year on which you have paid FICA or SECA payroll taxes, you cannot earn more than four (4) credits in any year. For example, if you earned $3,120 in January 2000, you would have earned four (4) credits and any earnings you may have thereafter would not give you any further credits because the first $3,120 (780 × 4) would have provided the total credits available for the year. While credits are tied to earnings, the number of credits does not have anything to do with the amount of benefits you or your family will receive. The excess earnings on which you pay FICA or SECA taxes will determine the monthly Social Security benefit. The number of credits, however, does establish whether you have a *fully insured* or *currently insured* status for Social Security benefits.

FULLY AND CURRENTLY INSURED STATUS

If you have earned 40 credits or quarters of coverage, you are considered *fully insured*. If you were born before 1929, you could be "fully insured" with fewer than 40 credits. For example, the SSA has stated that if you were born in 1925, only 36 credits would be required to be "fully insured"; in 1926 37 credits; in 1927, 38 credits; in 1928, 39 credits; and in 1929 and later, 40 credits.

You are also considered "fully insured" if you earned at least one credit for each year between the year in which you became 21 and the year in which you die or become disabled, provided at least six credits were earned.

Being "fully insured" qualifies you to receive your retirement benefits if you were in active military service before 1957 and do not have enough employment credits; your service may increase the credits to which you are entitled.

Serving in the Armed Forces has been considered covered employment by SSA since 1957 and FICA taxes have been withheld from military pay. If you were in active military service between 1940 and 1956, you are entitled to one (1) credit of Social Security coverage for each of the calendar year quarters you were in active service, provided you did not receive a dishonorable discharge. For each month you were in active service, $160 of earnings is credited even though no FICA taxes were paid during 1940 and 1956. They are used if needed to establish your insured status or to increase your benefit. However, you must inform the SSA and a determination must be made as to whether or not such credits are applicable in your case. A veteran, or next of kin if the veteran is deceased, has access to military records. The form to obtain a record of service is Request for Military Records #180 and can be obtained from:

National Personnel Records Center
9700 Page Boulevard
St. Louis, MO 63132
(314-263-3901)

This form is required by the SSA. The form also gives the recipient the addresses of the record depositories for the different services. The information obtained will provide the SSA with proof of your age, time of your service and record of service for the period. If you are receiving military retirement pay from the armed services because of disability, rather than length of service, you are entitled to credits for Social Security covering the same time period. This is important to veterans of Korea or Vietnam who may be entitled to Social Security Disability benefits in addition to the armed forces disability retirement benefits.

Being "fully insured" qualifies you and certain of your family members for some, but not all, Social Security benefits. For example, to receive retirement benefits, you only need to be "fully insured" and of the proper age. To receive disability benefits you may need to be both "fully insured" and have a disability status.

Survivors' benefits are payable to your surviving spouse and dependents based on your earnings record if you are "fully insured." It should be noted at this point that even if you should die with fewer credits than are required for retirement benefits, some of your survivors may be entitled to benefits if you are "currently insured."

Currently insured status is very important. You are considered currently insured if you have at least six credits in the 13-quarter period immediately before you die, or become entitled to either disability or retirement insurance benefits. Your surviving spouse may also be entitled to benefits if he or she is caring for entitled children who are under 16 or disabled, or if your surviving spouse is old enough to qualify for widow's or widower's benefits.

Average Monthly Social Security Benefits	
Average Monthly Benefit	**2000**
Retired workers	$804
Disabled workers and spouse with 1 or more children	$1255
Non-disabled widow(ers)	$775
Children of deceased workers	$512
Couple Both Receiving Benefits	$1348

Monthly and Yearly Percentage for Delayed Retirement Credits by Age		
Attain Age 65	**Monthly Percentage**	**Yearly Percentage**
Before 1982	1/12 of 1	1.0
1982–1989	1/4 of 1	3.0
1990–1991	7/24 of 1	3.5
1992–1993	1/3 of 1	4.0
1994–1995	3/8 of 1	4.5
1996–1997	5/12 of 1	5.0
1998–1999	11/24 of 1	5.5
2000–2001	1/2 of 1	6.0
2002–2003	13/24 of 1	6.5
2004–1005	7/12 of 1	7.0
2006–2007	5/8 of 1	7.5
2008 or after	2/3 of 1	8.0

Congress enacted The Contract With America Advancement Act (P.L. 104-121) in March 1996. It raised the *exempt amounts* under the annual earning test for persons who have reached the normal retirement age (currently 65) for the years 1997 to 2002 which beneficiaries may earn up to the following amounts and not have any benefits withheld:

> 1997 $13,500
>
> 1998 $14,500
>
> 1999 $15,500

This Act was repealed on April 7, 2000 by an Act of Congress retroactive to January 1, 2000.

Benefits were reduced by $1 for each $3 in earnings exceeding these amounts. After the year 2002, the annual exempt amount was indexed to the growth in average wages.

This Act also changed the annual exempt amount for persons under 65 to $10,080 for 2000. Benefits for such persons are reduced by $1 for each $2 of earnings above this amount.

The earnings test does not apply to beneficiaries aged 70 or over.

The maximum amount of earnings subject to FICA and SECA taxes increased from $72,600 for 1999 to $76,200 for 2000.

The Cost Of Living Adjustment applicable for 1999 benefits was fixed at 2.4%.

MAXIMUM FAMILY BENEFIT (MFB)

The Social Security Act places a limit on the total amount of benefits it will pay to a retired worker and dependents or survivors of the worker who may be entitled to benefits based on the worker's Primary Insurance Amount (PIA). This rule also applies to a disabled covered worker and dependents or survivors.

The SSA computes the average indexed monthly earnings (AIME) of the covered person and then determines the PIA by applying the following bend points for 1999 and percentages to the AIME: (Bend Points 1999 are $505 and $3,043)

Assume the AIME is $3,000. The SSA will make the following computation to arrive at the PIA:

On the first	$505 × 90%	$454.50
On next	2,538 × 32%	812.16
On next	43 × 15%	6.45
($3,000–$2,875)		
TOTAL is PIA		$1,273.11

Generally the MFB computed by the SSA will amount to approximately 150% to 180% of the PIA. If the total benefits payable to family beneficiaries exceed the MFB the SSA will deduct the worker's share of the benefits from the total being paid and then apportion the remaining benefits among the other beneficiaries.

Benefits to a divorced spouse or divorced widowed spouses are not counted as part of the family benefits and are not reduced to meet the allowable MFB.

COST-OF-LIVING ADJUSTMENTS

Cost of living adjustments, given each year, have, in recent years, been as low as 2.1%. (In 1981, it was 11.2%; in 1975 it was 8.0%.) In 2000, it is 2.4%.

CAN WE PRIVATIZE SOCIAL SECURITY?

In January 1997, President Clinton's Advisory Committee on Social Security issued a report that confused more than a few Americans. That confusion was due to the apparent inability of the committee to reach a consensus on what to do about the future of the Social Security program.

History indicated that Americans are a strange breed. When the government is confused, imaginative Americans undertake their own plans for retirement and from the report of the committee it appears that plans that have been effective are being ignored.

An option contained in the original Social Security Act of 1935 provided that local government employees could opt out of Social Security and design their own plan of retirement.

A number of counties in Texas in the 1980s designed such plans. The beauty of the plans was that the payroll tax that the Federal Government was taking from county employees for Social Security, 6.13%, at the time would now go into the Employees' Pension Fund and would be matched by the county's 6.13%. The plan contained the same employee benefits as Social Security—pensions and life and disability insurance. The life insurance benefit for those under 70 was 300% of annual earnings with a minimum benefit of $50,000 and a maximum of $150,000. Many had serious doubts about giving up Social Security benefits but when they came to retirement, they realized that the retirement benefits were higher than those they would have received under Social Security.

Many other counties recognized the benefits that growth of a private plan could provide, with many who retired after 20 years of service receiving three to four times what their ordinary Social Security benefits would have been.

Five states—California, Nevada, Maine, Ohio and Colorado—and many other local and state governments, have set up their own retirement systems in lieu of Social Security.

The government knows that these plans succeed. In 1984, the federal government set up the Thrift Savings Plan for government employees only and administered by Wells Fargo Funds. The plan's three funds now total $28 billion. Under the plan, if an employee making $35,000 per year invested 10% of his pay each year, after 30 years the employee would have more than $1.2 million in the retirement fund.

A number of House and Senate members and leading business persons and policy experts have made recommendations that place great emphasis on the creation of individual investment accounts.

Specifically such recommendations would require workers to put 2% of the 12.4% payroll tax paid into Social Security into individual investment accounts which they would be permitted to select from a number of investment options.

The appeal of such suggestion is based on the presumption that such accounts would give the recipient a higher level of benefits than under the present system. However, it should be noticed that market downturns or poor investment decisions could nullify such results.

In the author's opinion, if Social Security was privatized for all employees and the self-employed, benefits would be improved both for the individual and the government. The employer's share of the Social Security tax could be phased out over time and release approximately $170 billion per year to the business community, allowing the creation of more jobs and further stimulate the economy.

Why hasn't the Advisory Council on Social Security included these proven plans in its recommendations? It works for government employees, why not extend the benefits to all Americans.

TAXES AND OTHER MATTERS RELATING TO EARNINGS AND BENEFITS: SOCIAL SECURITY TAXES ON EARNINGS

The Federal Insurance Contributions Act (FICA) requires all employers and employees to pay the following taxes on wages and the Self-Employment Contributions Act (SECA) requires self-employed persons to pay taxes on all earnings from self-employment.

FICA Taxes

The FICA tax rate on earnings for 2000 is 7.65% up to a maximum of $76,200. The employer and employee must each pay this percentage of the worker's wages or a total of 15.3% which supports the payment of benefits

Summary of Social Security, Information
Effective January 1, 1999
Note: Some of these figures may change with the passage of the 1999 Budget Act. Check with the SSA at the number below.

Social Security and Medicare Tax Rates and Taxable Earnings

Tax Rates

Taxable Earnings	Employee/Employer	Self-Employed
Up to $76,200	*7.65% (each)	*15.3%
All earnings above $76,200	**1.45% (each)	**2.9%

*Combined Social Security and Medicare tax rate; Social Security portion is 6.20%.
**Medicare portion of Social Security tax.

Social Security Work Credits
(Also called quarters of coverage)

Work Credits	Earnings Required
One	$780
Four (maximum per year)	$3,120

Social Security Annual Earnings Limits

Age	Annual Earnings	Benefits Withheld
65–69	$17,000	$1 for every $3 exceeding limit
Under 65	$10,080	$1 for every $2 exceeding limit
70 or older	None	None

Supplemental Security Income (SSI)

Monthly Maximum	Individual	Couple
Basic Federal Payment	$512	$769
Income Limits:		
With earned income	$1,109	$1,623
With unearned income	$532	$789
Asset limits	$2,000	$3,000

TELEPHONE NUMBERS:		
	SOCIAL SECURITY	1-800-772-1213
	MEDICARE	1-800-638-6833
	INTERNET	http://www.ssa.gov.oact

for old age, survivors and disability recipients. All earnings above $76,200 are taxed an additional 1.45% for the Hospital Insurance Medicare Fund. The employer and employee must each pay this amount.

SECA Taxes

The SECA tax rate required to be paid by a self-employed person is 15.30% on the first $76,200 and 2.9% of all earnings over $76,200. A provision of the law permits the self-employed person to deduct 50% of the SECA taxes as an adjustment to total income.

Taxes on Social Security Benefits

If the only income you received in 1999 was Social Security, those benefits are not subject to taxes. If you have other income then some portion of Social Security benefits may be taxable as hereinafter provided. These rules apply to all residents of the United States whether citizens or immigrants. Nonresident aliens who may have received Social Security benefits are taxed on 85% of such benefits at a tax rate of 30%. If the income of a Social security beneficiary exceeds the *base amount* established for his or her status [i.e., (A) Single, (B) Married but filing separately, (C) Married and filing a joint tax return] then some portion of those Social Security benefits must be included as taxable income.

The 50% Rule

If the person's adjusted gross income (Line 31 of IRS Tax Form 1040) plus 50% of Social Security benefits, plus Tax Exempt Interest (referred to as modified adjusted gross income or MAGI) exceeds following base amounts (i.e., $25,000. if Single, Head of Household, a Widow(er) or Married Person Filing Separately and $32,000 if Married and Filing a Joint Tax Return) up to 50% of such benefit will have to be included as taxable income.

The 85% Rule

If the person's MAGI exceeds the base amount (i.e., $34,000 if Single, Head of

Example (A)
Single or Married Filing Separately
1. SOCIAL SECURITY BENEFIT 6,000
2. 50% of line 1 3,000
3. MAGI plus: Tax Exempt Interest 27,000
4. Total lines 2 and 3 30,000
5. Enter $25,000 base amount 25,000
6. Subtract line 5 from line 4 5,000
7. Taxable amount is 50% of the excess over the base amount, i.e., $2,500 or 50% of your Social Security benefit $3,000 whichever is the lesser amount.
8. Taxable amount of SS benefit: 2,500

Example (B)
Married Filing Jointly
1. SOCIAL SECURITY BENEFITS (joint) $10,000
2. 50% of line 5,000
3. MAGI plus Tax Exempt Interest 28,000
4. Total lines 2 and 3 31,000
5. Enter $32,000. 32,000
6. Subtract line 5 from line 4 –0–
None of the benefits are taxable.

Example (C)
Married, Filing Jointly
1. SOCIAL SECURITY BENEFITS (joint) $10,000
2. 50% of line 1 5,000
3. MAGI plus Tax Exempt Interest 42,000
4. Total lines 2 and 3 47,000
5. Enter $32,000 32,000
6. Subtract line 5 from 4 15,000
7. Enter difference between line 4 and $34,000 13000
8. Enter $12,000 if filing jointly 12,000
9. Subtract line 8 from 7 1,000
10. Enter lesser of line 7 or 8 12,000
11. Enter 50% of line 10 6,000
12. Enter lesser of line 2 or 11 5,000
13. Multiply line 9 by 85% 850
14. Add lines 12 and 13 5,850
15. Multiply line 1 by 85% 8,500
16. Taxable amount of benefits is the lesser of line 14 or 15 5,850

Household, a Widow(er), or Married Person Filing Separately and $44,000 if Married and Filing a Joint Tax Return) the amount of benefits included in gross income is 85% of the income over $44,000 plus the lesser of $6,000 or one-half of the benefits. However no more than 85% of benefits are subject to tax.

OTHER FACTORS THAT MAY AFFECT BENEFITS

The Social Security Law provides that when you start collecting Social Security benefits, you must report your earnings to the SSA annually. You will receive a form from SSA to report this because earnings may affect your benefits.

Only *earned income* is included in the determination affecting your benefits.

Earned income includes wages, tips, bonuses, commissions, fees, vacation pay, severance pay and sick pay. The reporting Form SSA-777-BK from SSA will explain these categories. If you have any doubt about what should be included, your local SSA office can supply the answer. Items that are not considered earned income are pensions not reported on your W-2 Form from the employer, interest, dividends, capital gains, annuities, gifts and inheritances, rental income, jury duty pay, Social Security and Veterans' benefits, royalties on pre-retirement copyrights or patents, retirement payments from a partnership and income from a limited partnership.

You are not required to file an annual report of earnings if you are receiving Social Security benefits but have no income that meets the SSA definition of earned income.

If you are 70 or older and receiving Social Security benefits, all earned income that you make is exempt from consideration and does not affect your benefits.

However if you are under 70 years of age and have earned income, your benefits will not be affected if your earnings are below the following limits:

1. If you are 70 for only part of the year, you need only report income earned

before the month in which you reached 70. If you are self-employed, divide your net annual earnings amount by 12 and report only the total for the months prior to reaching 70.

2. If you are between 65 and 69 the earnings limit is $17,000. If you earn more than this amount Social Security will withhold $1.00 for every $3.00 exceeding the limit.

3. If you are under 65 the earnings limit is $10,080. If you earn more than this amount Social Security will withhold $1.00 for every $2.00 exceeding the limit.

4. If you have exceeded the earnings limit and have been overpaid in your benefits for the prior year then Social Security will withhold such overpayment from your future benefit checks until the overpayment is recouped.

NONRESIDENT ALIENS

The internal revenue code provides that non-resident aliens who have income from U.S. investments will have 30% of that income withheld at the source for U.S. taxes.

If a nonresident alien qualifies for Social Security benefits, the IRS will require that 30% of one-half of those benefits be withheld for U.S. taxes.

CHANGES IN STATUS

Changes in a beneficiary's status may also affect the payment of benefits.

Social Security requires that all beneficiaries report the following changes in status:

1. If you are working and have or expect to have earnings in excess of the exempt earnings limitations.

2. If a person entitled to a child's, divorced spouse's, widow or widower's, or parent's benefit marries.

3. If a person under 62 receiving a mother's or father's benefit no longer has a child under age 16 or a disabled child under his or her care.

4. If a person receiving disability benefits has gone back to work or his or her con-

dition has improved so that the beneficiary is able to work.

5. If a child 18 or over receiving benefits as a student is no longer attending school fulltime.

6. Or when a person receiving benefit dies.

   NOTE: Failure to report such changes in status promptly may result in penalties. Promptly means within 3 months and 15 days after April 15 of the year following the close of the calendar year in which the change of status occurs.

EARNED INCOME TAX CREDIT (EITC)

If you are 65 or over, the internal revenue code provides that you are eligible for a credit equal to 15% of the base amount applicable to your filing situation.

The base amount is $5,000 if you are single or married and filing a joint return with only one spouse eligible. If you are married and filing a joint return with both spouses being eligible, the base amount is $7,500. The base amount for eligible married persons filing separate returns is $3,750.

This EITC credit is available if you are under 65 and retired with a permanent and total disability and have disability income from a public or private employer arising from such disability. In this case, the credit is limited to the amount of disability income (See IRS Schedule R (IRC 22).

NOTE: The Right to Work Act of 1996 not only established the level of earnings for 1997 that a beneficiary may attain without affecting Social Security benefits but also set the exempt amounts for beneficiaries age 65 to 70 for the following years as follows (this was repealed):

1998	$14,500
1999	$15,500
2000	$17,000
2001	$25,000

The levels for persons under 65 have not been set but will be released from year to year.

BILL SIGNING ENDS SOCIAL SECURITY EARNINGS CURB FOR RETIREES 65–69 RETROACTIVE TO JANUARY 1, 2000

Thousands of Americans age 65 through 69 will be able to earn as much money as they want without losing Social Security benefits under a bill signed Friday by President Clinton repealing a Depression-era penalty.

In addition, the repeal was retroactive to January 1, meaning that about 415,000 seniors who lost Social Security benefits this year will receive a refund. It will average $3,500 and be mailed out in May.

The measure repealed a law in which people age 65 to 69 lost $1 in Social Security benefits for every $3 in wages above an annual limit of $17,000. The cost of the repeal was estimated at $22 billion over 10 years.

Social Security is the largest federal benefit program, sending checks to 44 million Americans. Besides payments to retirees, Social Security also makes payments to disabled people and to survivors of workers who die young.

With Democrats and Republicans both eagerly counting the senior vote, the repeal sailed through Congress without dissent, approved by a 100-0 vote in the Senate and by 422-0 in the House.

CHAPTER TWO

Disability Insurance (DI)

DISABILITY INSURANCE (DI)

Disability insurance (DI) payments under OASDI cover a worker (and in a few cases, the worker's disabled widow or widower aged 50 or older, disabled adult child or grandchild aged 18 or older) who meets the program's qualifications for both eligibility and disability.

Disability benefits are also payable under SSI to severely disabled low-income people, including young children and others without a work history who are not eligible for DI benefits.

Disabled people who receive DI benefits become eligible for Medicare, usually after 24 months of receiving DI benefits. Children under 18 and spouses of disabled workers may be eligible for cash benefits. There is a waiting period of five full months which must pass before monthly payments may begin.

DEFINING DISABILITY

Disability is defined under SSA as a disabling condition, severe impairment physically or mentally of a person who is not able to perform "substantial gainful" activity or work. The impairment must be expected to last at least 12 months, or to result in death. The determination must be based on medical evidence.

These determinations are made on a case-by-case basis. The opinion of the attending physician (or physicians) is an important factor, but clinical and laboratory findings and other evidence of the severity

and probable duration of the disability are also taken into account.

An application must be made at the Social Security office when the disability first begins.

The local SSA office will first determine whether you meet a number of nondisability requirements such as whether you worked long enough in covered employment, your age (for disabled widow or widower benefits), or the relationship you have to a disabled worker if you are applying for benefits as a spouse or dependent child. If you meet the nondisability requirement, the application will be forwarded to the State's Disability Determination Service (DDS) to make the initial disability determination. The final decision regarding eligibility will be made by SSA.

The evaluation process for disability benefits covers the following:

■ Is the claimant doing "substantial" work? The SSA defines "substantial gainful activity" as performing significant mental or physical activities that are productive in nature. Work need not be full-time to be "substantial." Part-time work payments greater then the monthly exempt earnings amount for Social Security retirement beneficiaries are considered substantial. Earning $500 or more monthly is considered substantial and if an applicant is earning $500 or more a month, benefits are automatically denied. A "gainful" activity is something that is usually done in exchange for payment or wages, though it is not necessary that there be a profit or a wage in order for the activity to be considered gainful.

If benefits are not denied because of earning, the SSA will determine whether the claimant has a severe impairment that interferes with his or her ability to work.

- Severe impairment or impairments must be expected to last at least at least 12 months and must meet or equal the level of severity described in a "List of Impairments" as severely disabling. If the applicant has any of the conditions on this list, the disability claim is allowed.

- If the impairment does not meet or equal the SSA's listing of severe impairments even if it is expected to last at least 12 months and the impairment does not limit the claimant's ability to do the type of work he or she has been doing during the past 15 years, the claim will be denied.

- Finally, SSA will determine whether the claimant can do *any other work* based on the claimant's age, education, and work experience. Assuming the claimant cannot, then he or she is eligible for benefits.

ELIGIBILITY

A covered worker who is disabled at any age is eligible, and a disabled widowed spouse (and in some cases, a disabled surviving divorced spouse) is also eligible to collect these benefits on a covered worker's work record after the spouse reaches age 50.

Young people who become disabled before age 22 can begin collecting disability benefits at age 18 based on either the child's own work record or the work record of a retired, disabled, or deceased covered worker.

COVERED WORKERS

If you are age 31 or older, you need to qualify as fully insured and meet a recency of work test to be eligible for DI benefits. You must have a sufficient number of credits from work in covered employment to qualify as fully insured and a certain number of these credits must be earned in the years immedi-

ately preceding the onset of your disability. In most cases, meeting the recency of work test means that you have earned 20 credits during the 10 years preceding onset of your disability. (The blind do not have to meet the recency of work test.)

If you are disabled before age 31 but after 24, you will generally need credits equal to half of the total number of calendar quarters which have elapsed since you turned age 21, with a minimum of 6 credits.

- *Under 24:* If you are under 24 at the time you become disabled, you need credit of 1-1/2 years of work (6 credits) out of the 3-year period preceding the date of your disablement.

- *Between 24 and 31:* If your disability starts between ages 24 and 31, you need credit for having worked half of the time between age 21 and the time you become disabled. For example, to qualify at age 29, you would need to have worked for 4 out of 8 years (16 credits).

- *Age 31 and Older:* In this age group, you need the number of work credits shown in the next chart. Also, you must have earned at least 20 of these credits in the 10 years immediately before you become disabled.

Children who will be claimed as dependents on Internal Revenue Service returns must now have a Social Security number. Certain working and nonworking aliens who need to report income to the IRS must also have Social Security numbers.

DISABLED
WIDOWS AND WIDOWERS

A disabled widowed spouse, age 50 to 59, of a qualified worker is eligible for disability benefits on the basis of the deceased worker's earnings record. This spouse's benefit is 71.5% of the workers's primary insurance amount, and the benefit will not stop because of remarriage. However, a widow or widower must become disabled no later than

Born after 1929, disabled at age	Born before 1930, disabled at age 62:	Quarters of credit (& years) needed:
42 or younger		20 (5 years)
44		22 (5-1/2)
46		24 (6 years)
48		26 (6-1/2)
50		28 (7 years)
52	1981	30 (7-1/2)
53	1982	31 (7-3/4)
54	1983	32 (8 years)
55	1984	33 (8-1/4)
56	1985	34 (8-1/2)
58	1987	36 (9 years)
60	1989	38 (9-1/2)
62 or older	1991 or later	40 (10 years)

Note: If you are blind, credit may have been earned at any time: you need no recent credit.

seven years after the death of the worker to be eligible.

Over age 60, disabled widowed spouses may apply for a benefit called "Disabled Widow(er), Medicare only" benefits. This may enable you to receive Medicare benefits before age 65.

The same rules that define disability for a worker are applicable to widows and widowers. Divorced disabled surviving spouses may qualify for disability benefits on the work record of their former marriage partners provided the marriage to the worker on whose record the claim is made lasted for at least 10 years.

DISABLED CHILDREN

If a disabled adult child of a retired, disabled, or deceased covered worker is severely handicapped, physically or mentally, at any age prior to age 22, payments may start at age 18, provided the disability continues up to the date of the application for the benefit.

These benefits terminate at the death of the child or the end of the disability. They also terminate at marriage of the disabled adult child, unless the marriage is to another Social Security beneficiary age 18 or older. Disabled child benefits payable to a dependent, unmarried, *nondisabled* child terminate at age 18, or at 19 if a full-time student. They also end if the covered worker under whose record the benefit is being paid becomes unentitled to receive payments.

There is no age limit on filing an application for benefits as long as the disability began before age 22.

Benefit payments for a disabled *adult* child can be made only when a covered parent retires, becomes disabled, or dies.

A new disability standard for children under 18 was changed on August 22, 1996. A child will be considered disabled if the child has a "medically determinable impairment" which results in marked and severe functional limitations and which can be expected to last for a continuous period of not less than 12 months. The term of "maladjusted behavior" relating to children has been eliminated and use of individualized functional assessment in evaluating a child's disability is discontinued. (See Section on SSI-Current Recipient).

BLINDNESS

There are special provisions for blind persons applying for disability benefits. A blind person may be eligible to receive benefits under either the Social Security Disability program or under the Supplemental Security Income (SSI) program or both. DI eligibility means also becoming eligible for Medicare benefits after a waiting period. While the medical criteria are the same for both programs, the nonmedical criteria are not.

Social Security defines "blindness" as vision in your better eye of no better than 20/200 with corrective lenses, or limited to a visual field of 20 degrees or less even with corrective lenses. If you meet the disability eligibility criterion for DI, you do not have to meet the requirement for recent work.

You do need credits under Social Security for 2-1/2 years of work earned at any time before the application for disability benefits is made. Generally credits equal to the number of years after 1950, or age 21 if later, up to the year you are determined to be disabled because of blindness are considered. Blind people under 28 need no more than 6 credits. If you become legally blind at 41, you need 20 credits. No one needs more than 40 credits.

This compares with credit for 5 years of work in the 10 years preceding application for other disabled workers. Even if you do not meet this definition, you may still qualify if your disability prevents you from doing substantial work in 2000. There is a 5-month waiting period for benefit payment.

If you do continue to work and earn more than the maximum amount allowed, you should still apply for disability benefits. Even though you may not receive the benefits, your application is on file with the SSA and you can reapply if your earnings fall below the $1100 per month on your earnings record.

This means that these years of lower earnings will not be used to determine your average earnings for your Primary Insurance Amount and will not lower your primary benefit.

The legally blind are eligible for Medicare beginning at age 55.

ACQUIRED IMMUNE DEFICIENCY SYNDROME (AIDS)

Those with AIDS who are unable to work because of physical or mental impairment caused by the virus, and who meet the requirements of Social Security coverage described above, will qualify for Disability Insurance benefits.

People severely disabled with symptomatic Human Immunodeficiency Virus (HIV): pulmonary tuberculosis that resists treatment, Kaposi's sarcoma, pneumocystis carine pneumonia, carcinoma of the cervix, herpes simplex, Hodgkin's disease and all lymphomas, HIV wasting syndrome, candidiasis, pelvic inflammatory disease, condyloma, histoplasmosis, or retarded growth (in the case of children), may qualify.

As is generally true for other DI benefits, if you qualify for disability benefits because of AIDS or symptomatic HIV, the waiting period for payments to begin is 5 months from the onset of the disability. However, there is no waiting period for Supplemental Security Income (see SSI chapter), for which you may qualify. If you qualify for SSI, you may be eligible for Medicaid benefits to help cover the cost of treatment.

A guide to Social Security and SSI Disability Benefits for People with HIV Infection, is available from the SSA.

KIDNEY DISEASE

People of all ages with end-stage renal disease (permanent kidney failure) are usually eligible for Medicare, even if they are not eligible to receive DI benefits.

DRUG ADDICTION AND ALCOHOLISM

Effective March 29, 1996, Social Security and Supplemental Security Income (SSI) disability benefits are paid to people who are disabled because of drug and/or alcohol addiction. Enacted through law, this applies to people who are already getting benefits, and those who filed after August 1, 1996 for benefits because drug addiction and/or alcoholism prevents them from working. (See SSI, Drug Addiction or Alcoholism.)

The SSA pays benefits under both the Disability Insurance program and SSI. Both programs pay monthly benefits to people who are so severely disabled they can't work at any job. Under the this law:

- Your benefits must be paid to a "representative payee."
- You must undergo and make progress in appropriate treatment for your addiction or additions.
- You can receive disability benefits on the basis of your drug addiction and/or alcoholism for no more than 36 months.

The individual will not be deemed eligible for benefits if alcoholism or drug addiction is a contributing factor to disability.

Treatment Requirement

If you receive Social Security or SSI disability benefits because of drug addiction and/or alcoholism, you are required to receive treatment for your disability. The SSA will refer you to an agency that will decide what treatment is appropriate for your condition and determine if treatment is available. That agency will also verify whether you go for and make progress in available treatment.

Payments will stop if that person refuses to accept rehabilitation treatment without good cause.

Under present law, you may receive benefits for no more than 36 months. The SSA will notify the beneficiary before the 36-month period ends as to when the benefits will stop.

Representative Payee

Benefits paid because of drug addiction and/or alcoholism (along with some other situations and conditions) must be sent to a representative payee, who manages the money for the beneficiary. This representative payee may be a non-profit social service agency, a governmental social service agency or public guardian, another organization, or a family member the SSA approves to act in the best interest of the beneficiary.

DISABILITY BENEFITS

Disability benefits are based on average indexed monthly earnings.

If you are age 65 or over when you become disabled, you will receive the full retirement benefits to which you are entitled instead of disability benefits. But if you are under 65, your benefits may be reduced by Worker's Compensation or by any disability payments you get from federal, state, or local programs.

A disabled widowed spouse over 60 receives the same survivors' benefit as a widowed spouse (based on 100% of the worker's primary benefit).

A disabled widowed spouse aged 60 to 64 claiming a benefit will have her (or his) payment reduced by .475% for each month before age 65. A disabled widowed spouse between ages 50 and 60 has her (or his) benefit reduced to 71.5% of the deceased worker's PIA. (A disabled widowed spouse under 50 is too young for a widow(er)'s benefit—unless she or he is caring for a qualified minor child—but could still be eligible for her or his own disability benefit.) The same benefits apply to divorced widowed spouses, provided they were married to the worker for at least 10 years.

If you become disabled, your dependent family members are eligible for benefits of the same percentage of your PIA that they would be entitled to when you retire. The maximum family benefit, however, is lower for DI than it is for retirement and survivors' benefits. As a general rule, the maximum for DI is 150% of the worker's PIA, but it can be as low as 100%.

ELIGIBILITY FOR OTHER PAYMENTS

If you are a Social Security disability beneficiary, you should know that benefits from some other sources may affect your disability check.

Disability benefits are not payable in full if you receive another Social Security check. If you are entitled to more than one monthly benefit, the amount you receive usually will be equal to the larger of the 2 amounts.

If a spouse has been receiving a retirement or disability payment which is larger than the spouse's benefit rate, he or she will receive only one—the retirement or the disability benefit.

A reduction method for disability was instituted to avoid windfall benefits to some workers. Before the reduction became effective, some Social Security beneficiaries received more in combined public disability payment than they had been earning when they were working.

If you are a disabled worker under 65 and also receive disability payments from other government programs, combined payments to you and your family are limited. Payments usually cannot exceed 80% of your average current earnings before you became disabled. And all earnings covered by Social Security, including amounts above the maximum taxable by Social Security, may be considered when figuring average earnings.

DISABILITY REVIEWS (CDR'S)

If you are already receiving disability benefits, they could be reduced or eliminated after review. The Social Security Administration is required by law to periodically review the status of Social Security disability beneficiaries to determine if they continue to be disabled.

- Medical improvements expected—beneficiary's status generally scheduled for review within 6-18 months of the most recent medical decision.
- Medical improvement possible—beneficiary's status scheduled for review no sooner than every 3 years.
- Medical improvement not expected—beneficiary's status scheduled for review no sooner than every 7 years.

This procedure includes an in-depth field office interview, evaluation of the medical evidence of record by a State Disability Determination Service (DDS) examiner, and a possible consultative medical exam to obtain any additional information needed to assess the possibility of medical improvement of the beneficiary's present condition. A full medical CDR process requires an in-person appearance by the beneficiary. It places a considerable burden both on the disabled beneficiary and on SSA in order to determine the beneficiary's continuing eligibility.

When your case comes up for CDR, you must be notified and informed that you have the right to submit medical or other evidence for consideration. If the SSA decides that your disability benefits should be terminated, it must give you a written notice that explains your right to appeal.

APPEALS OF DECISIONS

About 1.5 million people will file for Social Security disability benefits this year. A substantial number of these applications will be denied at some point in the application process, but if you have a sound basis for an appeal, the denial may be reversed.

If you receive a decision you disagree with, what can you do:

The answer is to file an appeal. Every decision Social Security makes is subject to review.

APPLICATION FOR DISABILITY BENEFITS

Determining eligibility for DI benefits requires all the same information necessary for an application for retirement benefits. You can help expedite the process in a number of ways.

Once you apply for benefits, contact your medical providers to see whether they are sending out the necessary records for your disability review. Also, it will help to have the following information available when you file for benefits.

Social Security Number

For you, your spouse, and any dependents applying for benefits. You also will need proof of age.

Any number(s) on which you or your dependents receive (or received) Social Security checks.

Impairment Information

What it is and when it started.

How it keeps you from working.

How it affects your daily activities.

Treatment Information

The names, addresses (including zip code), and telephone and fax numbers of all doctors, hospitals, or other medical facilities where you have been treated or tested.

Any medical reports in your possession from doctors, hospitals, laboratories, clinics and caseworkers. SSA will make copies of these records and return them to you.

Dates of medical visits and types of treatment or tests.

Hospital or clinic account number, or DVA claim number for any other disability benefits you receive or have applied for.

Any medications you are taking: names, dosage, and frequency.

Any restrictions a physician has placed on your activities.

Work History

■ Date you stopped working.

■ If you are working now, date you returned to work, employer, and information about your current job.

■ Summary of where you worked during the past 15 years and the kind of work you did.

■ A copy of your latest W-2 Form (Wage and Tax Statement) or, if self-employed, your federal tax return for the past year.

Take all this documentation to your local Social Security office where you will make your formal application.

If your disability prevents you from filing your claim at your local office, you may be able to file it over the telephone or by mail. You can have a Social Security caseworker come to where you are to complete your application. If you are unable to file it yourself, your application can be made by your spouse, a relative, or a friend.

The information you provide is sent to your state Disability Determination Service (DDS) for evaluation and a decision. There is a 5-month waiting period before you become eligible to receive monthly benefits.

If you wish to apply for Social Security disability benefits, call Social Security's toll-free number, 1-800-772-1213, any day between 7 A.M. and 7 P.M. and ask for the *Disability* booklet.

BENEFITS FOR PEOPLE WITH DISABILITIES WHO WORK

Special rules make it possible for people with disabilities receiving Social Security or Supplemental Security Income (SSI) to work and still receive monthly cash payments and Medicare or Medicaid. Social Security calls these rules "work incentives." The rules are different for Social Security and SSI beneficiaries. Following are the rules that apply under each program.

Social Security

Trial Work Period

For nine months (not necessarily consecutive), a disabled or blind Social Security beneficiary's earnings will not affect his or her Social Security benefit.

Extended Period of Eligibility

For three years after a successful trial work period, a disabled or blind Social Security beneficiary may receive a disability check for any month during which his or her earnings are not at a substantial gainful activity level.

Continuation of Medicare

If Social Security disability payments stop because you are earning at the substantial gainful activity level but you are still disabled, Medicare can continue for up to 39 months after the trial work period.

Impairment-Related Work Expenses

Certain expenses for things a disabled person needs because of his or her impairment in order to work may be deducted when counting earnings to determine if the person is performing substantial gainful activity.

Recovery During Vocational Rehabilitation

If you recover while participating in a vocational rehabilitation program that is likely to lead to becoming self-supporting, benefits may continue until the program ends.

Special Rules for Blind Persons

Several special rules apply to blind beneficiaries who work. Ask at the Social Security office for details on work incentives for blind beneficiaries.

Supplemental Security Income (SSI)

Continuation of SSI

Disabled or blind SSI recipients who work may continue to receive payments until countable income exceeds SSI limits.

Continuation of Medicaid Eligibility

Medicaid may continue for the disabled or blind SSI recipients who earn over the SSI limits if the person cannot afford similar medical care and depends on the Medicaid in order to work.

Plan for Achieving Self-Support (PASS)

A disabled or blind SSI recipient may set aside income and resources for up to 48 months toward an approved plan for achieving self-support.

Impairment-Related Work Expenses

Certain expenses for things a disabled person needs because of his or her impairment in order to work may be deducted when counting earnings to determine if the person continues to be eligible. For blind persons who work, the work expenses need not be related to the impairment.

Recovery During Vocational Rehabilitation

If a person recovers while participating in a vocational rehabilitation program that is likely to lead to becoming self-supporting, benefits may continue until the program ends.

Sheltered Workshop Payments

Pay received in a sheltered workshop is treated as earned income, regardless of whether it is considered wages for other purposes. This enables Social Security to exclude more of the sheltered workshop employee's earnings when computing his or her SSI payment.

Disabled Students

Tuition, books and other expenses related to getting an education may not be counted as income for recipients who go to school or are in a training program.

Social Security Special Notes

All children who will be claimed dependents on internal revenue returns must have a Social Security number. Hospitals have made arrangements for the appropriate application forms for the new mother and father to apply for the Social Security number when the child is born. Ask your hospital for the forms or obtain them at your local Social Security office.

Direct Deposit of Social Security Checks and Other Government Payments (Except Tax Refunds)

Congress enacted a law in 1997 requiring all Federal Disbursements to be made to beneficiaries by electronic funds transfer (EFT) effective January 2, 1999 (for those who have bank accounts). Such persons must make arrangements with their respective banks to have their checks directly deposited to the bank account.

Those without bank accounts, or who have disabilities or other circumstances that create a real hardship in receiving such checks by EFT can apply to their local Social Security office for a waiver.

The government has provided that persons without bank accounts are exempted from EFT requirements until January 2, 2000, recognizing that many persons without bank accounts cannot afford the bank fees and the government is reviewing the possibility of a plan to offer such persons special accounts at a federally insured financial institution at low cost. Check with your local Social Security office for such alternative.

CHAPTER THREE

Medicare

MEDICARE

Medicare is a national health insurance program that was enacted in 1965 to provide health insurance for people 65 years of age and older, qualified younger disabled persons and those with kidney failure.

The program is divided into two parts; *hospital insurance* (Part A) and *medical insurance* (Part B).

Part A helps pay for care in a hospital and skilled nursing facility services, home health and hospice care.

Part B helps pay doctors' bills, outpatient hospital care and some medical services not covered by Part A. The statement "helps pay for" is important. Neither Part A nor Part B pays all bills.

You will notice later on in our discussion that there are hospital "deductible amounts" that you are required to pay during any "benefit period." A benefit period begins when you are admitted to a hospital and ends when you have been out of the hospital or skilled nursing facility for 60 straight days. The next time you are admitted to a hospital, a new benefit period begins. There is no limit on the number of benefit periods you may have.

Under Part B, you are responsible for paying the first $100 each year of the charges approved by Medicare. This charge is referred to as the Part B deductible. After the deductible has been met by you, Medicare will pay 80% of the Medicare approved amount of most services and you will be responsible for the 20%.

At this point, you should be aware that the current regulations permit *a doctor who does not accept assignment* to bill the patient for the "approved amount" plus 15% (for example, if the Medicare-approved amount for the doctors services is $200, the doctor can bill the patient up to $230 for the services). Any over-charges should be refunded if the patient has paid in advance.

Some doctors *will accept assignment* to accept the "Medicare Approved" amount in full payment for services rendered and the patient is not required to pay any amount in excess of 20% of the "approved amount." Ask your doctor if he or she accepts assignment before services are rendered.

The part of the bill that is not paid by Medicare is called *coinsurance* and any amount that you pay as such coinsurance is counted toward your annual deductible of $100.

You may want to buy *Medigap insurance* to help pay the deductible and coinsurance amounts that Medicare does not pay. See the section on Medigap policies for availability or timing on such purchases.

For persons with limited income and resources, there is a qualified Medicare beneficiary (QMB) Program that will pay the full Medicare Medical Insurance (Part B) monthly Medicare premium and all deductible and coinsurance expenses for such persons. Check with the Local Social Security Office for such benefits.

ENROLLMENT

Enrollment in Medicare can occur in two ways. If you are already receiving Social Security Retirement benefits when you reach

65, you do not have to apply for Medicare. You are automatically enrolled in Part A Hospital and Part B Medical insurance and your Medicare Card is mailed to you within three months before your 65th birthday. If you have been receiving Disability benefits under Social Security for 24 months, you, too, will receive your Medicare Card automatically.

If you are not receiving Social Security benefits, then three months before you reach 65 years of age, apply for Medicare at your local Social Security office. Your Initial Enrollment Period for Medicare starts three months before you reach 65 and continues for seven months. Apply early and avoid a delay in the start of your coverage.

If you do not enroll during this seven-month period, you will have to wait until the next General Enrollment Period which will be held January 1 to March 31 of each year but coverage will not start until July following enrollment.

Do not put off enrollment. If you wait twelve months or more to sign up, your premiums will be higher. Part B premiums go up $10 for each 12 months that you could have enrolled and failed to do so. The Part A Hospital premium is 10% no matter how late you apply for coverage.

When you enroll for Part A Hospital coverage, it is recommended that you also enroll for Part B Medical at the same time regardless of other insurance that you may be carrying.

The Health Care Financing Administration (HCFA) directs the Medicare and Medicaid Programs.

Medicare is generally the Secondary Payer of Hospital and Medical expenses if you are covered by an employer insurance plan, veterans benefits, workman's compensation or other insurance.

It should be noted at this time that Medicare will not pay for care received from a hospital, skilled nursing facility, home health agency or hospice that is "not certified" to participate in the Medicare program, except that Medicare will help pay for care in a non-participating hospital if the patient is admitted to such hospital for emergency treatment and the nonparticipating hospital is the closest one equipped to handle the emergency. Emergency treatment is defined as treatment that is immediately necessary to prevent death or serious impairment to the patient's health.

ELIGIBILITY

You are automatically eligible for hospital insurance:

- **At age 65,** if you are entitled to monthly Social Security benefits, even though you may still be working and not collecting benefits.

- **At age 65,** or over, if you are the widow or widower of a person who was entitled to Social Security benefits.

- **Under 65,** if you have been entitled to Social Security disability insurance benefits for 24 months. In some cases, disabled government employees and certain family members are eligible for Medicare after 29 months of disability.

- **At any age,** if you are fully or currently insured with Social Security (See Chapter 2) and need maintenance dialysis or a kidney transplant (coverage starts the third month after you begin dialysis).

When you apply for your retirement benefits at age 65, you also apply for both parts of Medicare.

If for some reason you are not eligible for Medicare at age 65, you can purchase it through voluntary enrollment. To qualify for voluntary enrollment, you must be 65 or over, live in the United States, and be a U.S. citizen. Aliens are also eligible, if legally admitted and residing in the United States continuously for 5 years immediately prior to Medicare enrollment.

If you voluntarily enroll in Part A, you must also take Part B, the Supplementary Medical Insurance. However, you can enroll in Part B without taking Part A.

The 2000 monthly premium for voluntary enrollees in Medicare Part A is $301 with less than 30 quarters of coverage, $166 with 30 quarters or more. The HCFA will bill you for this coverage on a monthly basis.

SERVICES COVERED BY PART A

Medicare hospital insurance covers these services: hospital, skilled nursing facility, post-hospital home health agency, hospice care, and blood replacement. In addition, Medicare Part A also covers a maximum of 190 days per lifetime for inpatient psychiatric hospital care. Drug and alcohol rehabilitation may be covered under this psychiatric provision, or it may be covered under regular hospitalization or disability provisions, depending on the circumstances of admission.

Benefit Periods and Reserve Days

Medicare calculates use of its hospital coverage in "benefit periods" and "reserve days." Understanding these terms helps to untangle the rules governing the length and frequency of hospital stays and the deductibles that apply to different situations.

Benefit Periods

A benefit period begins on the day you enter the hospital and ends when you have been out of the hospital (or other covered facility) for 60 consecutive days. For example, if you are admitted to the hospital on March 3 and discharged on March 15, Medicare pays all but $776 of the bill. You pay the $776; this is your deductible—and you will have used 12 days of that benefit period.

Then, if you are readmitted to the hospital on April 1 for 4 days, you will be within the same benefit period and will use up another 4 days of it but will not have to pay the $776 for that benefit period again.

If, however, you are not readmitted until August (more than 60 days after you left the hospital), the benefit period will not be the same as the one that began in March, and you will have to pay the $776 for a new benefit period.

Reserve Days

With the exception of hospice care, there are no limits on the number of benefit periods that you may use, but if you have to stay in the hospital for more than 90 days, the days beyond the 90th day fall into a special category called "reserve days."

Hospital Benefits

During each and every benefit period that you use, Medicare will pay one amount (all but the $776 mentioned above for 2000) toward the first 60 days of a hospital stay. Medicare will pay a lesser amount toward the next 30 days (all covered inpatient services except for $194 a day). After that you may use some or all of your reserve days, for which Medicare pays for all covered services except $388 a day.

As a Medicare beneficiary, you are entitled to only 60 reserve days in a lifetime. Though you may use them a few days at a time, once they are used up, these reserve days are not renewable. You may decide whether or not you want to use any of your reserve days in any given situation; if you decide you do not want to use them, you must notify the hospital *in writing* before the 90th day, or any days beyond 90 automatically will be considered reserve days.

PPS and DRG's

Hospitals are paid by Medicare, not on the basis of what they charge, but by what is called the Prospective Payment System (PPS). Under this system, there is a predetermined standard rate, or average cost, for particular categories of treatment. The fixed fees vary among the 9 regions of the nation and between rural and urban facilities, but a single payment is made for each type of case, as it is identified by the Diagnosis Related Group or DRG. There are 468 groups designated for classification of particular cases.

Each DRG specifies the length of hospital stay for the determined condition. If the hospital keeps you longer than the DRG for your condition allows, the hospital bears the extra cost. If you are released before your DRG time limit is up, the hospital is still paid the same amount.

Skilled Nursing Facility Care (SNF)

If you meet the following conditions, Medicare can pay for your rehabilitation care in a skilled nursing facility:

- You need daily skilled nursing or rehabilitation services which are best provided in an SNF and this need is certified by a medical professional.
- You were in a hospital for at least 3 days in a row and are entering the SNF shortly (usually within 30 days) after being discharged from the hospital.
- You will be treated in the SNF for the same condition that was treated in the hospital.

Medicare Part A (HI) will pay for the first 20 days of care in an SNF. From days 21 through 100, Medicare will pay for all covered services, except for $97.00 a day. (Medicare Part B will cover many of the physician services.)

Home Health Care Services

Under certain conditions, Medicare Part A or B will pay all the cost of limited skilled healthcare in your home-including skilled nursing care, physical therapy, and speech therapy. It does not, however, cover services such as meal preparation, shopping, laundry or other housekeeping chores, generally referred to as "custodial care."

Medicare and Medigap policies do not provide substantial protection from expenses arising from long-term care in the home or in institutions such as nursing homes. Medicare and Medigap fund some short-term rehabilitation services in skilled nursing facilities (up to 100 days per stay) and some lim-ited home health services. But there is no long-term protection for nursing home or community-based long-term care. Medicaid and Veterans Administration health programs sometimes cover a substantial portion of such services.

Hospice Care

Hospices provide supportive service for the terminally ill, who may elect to receive them instead of standard Medicare benefits. Hospice care may be delivered at home or in an institution, and, in addition to pain management and counseling, includes housekeeping services when the patient is at home.

Assignment

The easiest way to deal with Medicare is to choose doctors and suppliers who "accept assignment," that is, take the approved Medicare charge as full payment. The patient is then responsible only for the 20% of the approved charge Medicare does not pay, the deductible, and any services not covered. Not all physicians accept assignment, and there are some who accept assignment only for some services.

Even though your physician or supplier does not accept assignment, there are limits on the amount you can be charged above the set fee for that service. For 2000, check with your local Social Security office for the current limits on accepted charges for office and hospital visits, surgery, and other services. Severe penalties are imposed for charging fees above the limits.

You can find out which doctors in your area accept assignment of claims by checking the physicians' directory for your state which is published by your area insurance carrier. Your local Social Security office has this book, as do most agencies for seniors. Acceptance of assignment by your doctor will save you money and paperwork.

The regulations of the Social Security Act does not permit a doctor who does not accept assignment to bill the patient for more than 15% of the "approved amount" (e.g., if the Medicare-approved amount for the doctors services is $200, a doctor can bill the patient up to $230 for the services). Any over-charges should be refunded if the patient has paid in advance.

SERVICES NOT COVERED BY PART A

Medicare will not pay for anything that isn't "medically reasonable and necessary." For example, Medicare will not pay for your television or telephone fees while you are in the hospital. For the most part, your doctor determines what is medically reasonable and necessary, and the hospital's utilization review committee and the area Peer Review Organization monitor the doctor's decision.

There are some other things, as well, for which Medicare hospital insurance will *not* pay:

- Custodial care as provided by most nursing homes.
- Full-time nursing care in your home.
- Private room and private-duty nursing (unless medically necessary).
- Services paid for by other forms of insurance, such as workers' compensation, automobile or other liability insurance, or employer health plans.
- Charges for services in excess of the Medicare standards.
- Items or services for which you are not legally obligated to pay. There are some charges for services which Medicare may refuse to pay that you do not have to pay either.
- Drugs and treatments the Food and Drug Administration has not found "safe and effective" and out-patient prescription drugs.
- Hospital treatment in a foreign country. The exception to this is for treatment of an emergency that occurred in the United States and the foreign hospital is closer than one in the United States, or if the emergency occurred in transit between the continental United States and Alaska.

If you have a question about whether or not any item is covered, you can telephone the insurance intermediary for your area and ask. Or you can submit the claim and see what happens.

COPAYMENTS AND DEDUCTIBLES FOR PART A

Copayments are the payments that you, or whatever health insurance you carry in addition to Medicare, must make to cover expenses that Medicare does not pay. Charges for the Medicare approved services (such as the $776 of the hospital bill at the beginning of a benefit period you have to cover before Medicare begins paying) count toward your deductible.

SIGNING UP FOR MEDICARE, PARTS A AND B: ENROLLMENT PERIODS

You must decide whether or not you want Medicare coverage and enroll during one of 3 enrollment periods.

The first opportunity is called the "initial enrollment period." This period begins 3 months before the month you become eligible and ends 3 months after that—7 months in all. For example: if your 65th birthday is in August, you become eligible in July, so your initial enrollment period would run from April 1 through October 31 of that same year. If you sign up in April, May, or June, your medical insurance begins in July. If you enroll between July and the end of October, coverage starts 1 to 3 months after you have enrolled.

Should you decide later that you want Medicare coverage and your initial enrollment period has passed, you have a second opportunity: you can sign up during the general enrollment period, which runs from January 1 through March 31 of each year. Your coverage will not begin until the following July, and you will have to pay a surcharge. Your monthly premium will go up 10% for every year you were eligible and did not enroll.

If you work past 65 and have employer health coverage, or if you are 65 and your spouse is a worker of any age, the third opportunity to enroll is during a "special enrollment period" consisting of the 7 months beginning with the month your group coverage ends, or the month employment ends, whichever is first. You do not have to wait for a general enrollment period or pay the surcharge, but you have to meet certain requirements. Check with your Social Security office or your employer's benefits office.

SAFEGUARDS AGAINST ABUSES

Peer Review Organizations have been set up by the HCFA to review complaints regarding Medicare admissions, discharges of patients, and performance or medical procedures. These PROs, as they are called, have the authority to hold hospitals and doctors responsible for violating rules regarding admissions, premature discharges, and performance (or lack of performance) of medical procedures.

Certainly there are instances of fraud in the system, and many more of outright waste. We all pay for it ultimately, so it deserves reporting. The PRO for your area is listed in *The Medicare Handbook* along with full instructions for reporting abuses. Addresses for reporting fraud and abuses also appear in Appendix A.

APPEALS RELATING TO HOSPITAL, HOSPICE, OR HOME CARE

Should you or your physician believe Medicare is terminating your hospital, hospice, SNF, or home care too soon, you can appeal this decision to your PRO when Medicare sends you a Notice of Noncoverage. If you request the review by noon of the first day after receipt of the notice, your Medicare coverage is automatically extended and you will not have to pay until the PRO makes its decision. If, however, the PRO is reviewing the matter for a second time, you may have to pay for the time you spend in the hospital or hospice while the decision is being made—usually no more than a day. The steps to take for making an appeal is set forth in the section on appeals.

MEDICARE PART B: MEDICAL INSURANCE

Medicare Part B, medical insurance, is also called voluntary Supplementary Medical Insurance (SMI) and is financed by payments from the federal government and by monthly premiums paid by people enrolled in the plan. Part B helps pay for doctors' bills, diagnostic tests, outpatient hospital care, medical equipment, ambulance services, and other medical services and supplies not covered by Part A.

PART B APPLICATION AND ENROLLMENT

You can enroll for Part B medical insurance in 3 different ways:

- You are automatically enrolled if you apply for and receive Social Security. You must pay a monthly premium for this coverage. However, if you do not wish to have the coverage, you must say so at the time you become eligible for hospital insurance (Medicare Part A).
- You can voluntarily enroll for Part B if you are over 65. You do not have to be entitled to Social Security benefits in order to get this coverage, but you must pay monthly premiums for it. You may enroll for *both* Parts A and B, but if you prefer, you may enroll in Part B only.
- If you were a disability insurance beneficiary who lost your Part A coverage because you returned to work, you may be able to purchase Medicare Part A and B coverage.

Enrollment for Medicare Part B is automatic if you apply for and receive Social Security benefits. Enrollment in Medicare Part B is automatic 24 months after benefits start for those receiving disability insurance. Otherwise, you have to apply for enrollment in medical insurance if:

- You plan to work past 65.
- You are 65 but ineligible for hospital insurance.
- You have permanent kidney failure.
- You are a disabled widow or widower between 50 and 65 and you are not receiving disability checks.

NOTE: There are "enrollment periods" for Medicare (both or either parts), during which you must sign up or pay a penalty in the form of a higher premium if you are late. Exceptions to these rules are made for some situations in which there is coverage from employment, or when that coverage changes. See your *Medicare Handbook* for details, or call your Medicare insurance carrier.

PART B PREMIUMS

The monthly Part B premium for 2000 is $45.50. As mentioned earlier, this premium is slightly lower than the 1999 premium, and if you are already on Medicare, you received an explanation for this increase with your first billing notice for 2000.

This premium is deducted from your Social Security check. If you do not receive a benefit check, you are billed for the premium on a quarterly basis.

If you find you are unable to pay your premium, call your local Social Security office and give the reason for your nonpayment. If your explanation is accepted, you will be given a grace period—usually 90 days—in which to pay the premium. However, if you do not pay within the grace period, your coverage will be canceled and future reinstatement will result in a higher premium. You might also look into the QMB and SLMB programs discussed at the beginning of this chapter.

REQUIREMENTS FOR DEDUCTIBLE AND APPROVED CHARGES

In order to receive medical insurance benefits from Medicare, you must first pay the annual deductible, and Medicare must have approved the charge for each category of service you have received.

Deductible for Part B

For calendar year 2000, you must pay the first $100—the deductible—of your doctor or medical bills. (Your other health insurance may pay some or all of this deductible; it may also have its own deductible.) Don't wait until your bills total the amount of the Medicare deductible; submit individual bills as you pay them so they will be applied to your deductible. Meeting this deductible is a one-time requirement for each calendar year.

You also have an annual blood deductible; you can either pay for the first three pints of blood you use or replace them. Blood is covered under both Parts A and B, but the deductible has to be met only once under either part in a calendar year. Medicare will pay 80% of the cost of blood in excess of three pints.

Coinsurance (Cost Sharing)

After the deductible is met, Medicare still pays only part of the bill; you or your other insurance must pay the rest. Broadly speaking, the coinsurance for Part A is the specified amount that you (or your other insurance) pay after Medicare has paid its limit in each benefit period. For Part B, your share of the cost is the amount beyond Medicare's 80% of the approved charge; that is, you are responsible for 20% plus anything else you are obliged to pay beyond the approved charge.

Recognized, Approved, or Allowable Charges

After you have paid the deductible for the calendar year, Medicare Part B will make 80% of the payments toward certain expenses above the deductible. These payments are not based on your doctors' bills or your medical suppliers' charges, but are based instead on what Medicare defines as reasonable, allowable, or the "approved charge" under the new fee schedule.

General Information: PART B

More Medicare benefits. Medicare has added benefits to help you stay healthy. These benefits now include: flu and pneumococcal pneumonia shots (Medicare pays 100%), pap smears, including pelvis and breast exam and yearly mammograms (no Part-B deductible); and colorectal cancer screening. Talk to your doctor to see if these benefits are right for you. Even more Medicare benefits will be available in 2000. Look for more information.

Resource-Based Relative-Value System (RBRV)

Finding a way to arrive at fair and reasonable approved charges for physicians is an ongoing struggle; the introduction of a new fee schedule called the Resource-Based Relative-Value system, or RBRV, is the latest attempt to satisfy all parties. It has drawn a great deal of criticism from the American Medical Association.

The purpose of the plan is to introduce greater equality in payments among different kinds of physicians. The new fee schedule has had the effect of giving more money to general practitioners and less to specialists. It has also cut Medicare expenditures.

Under the RBRV plan, a number is assigned to a treatment (from 1 for an office visit to 119 for a liver transplant) with a dollar figure tied to the number. The more complex the treatment is, the higher the number. The doctor's or other provider's overhead and liability insurance premiums are also figured into this system.

Medicare is not the only form of insurance this fee schedule effects. Many large health insurance carriers have adopted the RBRV system for their healthcare policies as well.

As long as medical costs continue to rise faster than the overall inflation rate, and as long as a large percentage of Americans can-

not afford adequate medical care—or the insurance to pay for it—there will be controversy about how health providers are paid. This controversy will express itself in frequent policy changes in Medicare—changes that will affect the entire American healthcare system.

SUBMITTING PART B MEDICARE CLAIMS

Medicare providers under Part B are now required to prepare and submit Medicare claims for their patients. They have to do this whether or not the provider of the services or supplies accepts assignment. The providers are also prohibited by law from charging any fee for filling out and submitting these claims.

The provider submits the claim to the insurance carrier, and the carrier pays 80% of the approved charge directly to the provider; you are responsible for paying the rest. Claims should be submitted promptly; most providers do so, since it is in their best interest as well as yours. (Most providers now submit Medicare claims electronically, some will also submit Medigap claims at the same time.)

The rule that providers have to handle the submission of claims doesn't mean that you will never have to make a claim yourself. In some cases, you may have to do so. The necessary forms can be obtained from your local Social Security office.

PRIMARY AND SECONDARY PAYERS

If you have health insurance through an employer, it is your primary insurance and this insurer pays first; Medicare is the secondary payer. If this is your situation, your provider may not be required (or might not choose) to make the claim for you. Since the primary payer has to pay before Medicare will, you may have to file one or both of these claims. When you have supplementary insurance (Medigap), and Medicare is your primary payer, all providers must prepare the necessary paperwork to support the charges and file the claim with the Medicare carrier. This is the case even if the supplier is not a Medicare participant. Examples of this situation would be a payment for emergency treatment in a Canadian or Mexican hospital, or a U.S. hospital or HMO (Health Maintenance Organization) that is not in the Medicare system. Such suppliers may not make the supplementary claim to your Medigap insurer; you will have to do that yourself.

If the doctor accepts assignments on a Part B claim, and you have signed the form giving that doctor the right to submit claims on your behalf, the Medicare carrier or the doctor may submit claims to your Medigap insurer.

SERVICES COVERED BY PART B

After you have paid the first $100 (the deductible) of approved or recognized charges for the covered services provided, supplementary medical insurance will pay 80% of the covered expenses, subject to the maximum charges of the fee schedule. Among the services covered are:

Physician's services, including surgery and anesthesia, either outpatient or inpatient, and no matter where received, at home, doctor's office, clinic or in a hospital and supplies furnished as part of the service.

X-rays and laboratory tests.

Ambulance transportation when deemed necessary.

Breast prostheses following a mastectomy.

Services of certain specially qualified practitioners who are not doctors.

Physical and occupational therapy.

Speech language pathology services.

Home healthcare, if you do not have Part A of Medicare.

Blood, after the first three pints.

Flu, pneumonia and hepatitis B shots.

Pap smears for the detection of cervical cancer (some limitations by age and risk).

Mammograms to screen for breast cancer.

- Outpatient mental health services.
- Artificial limbs and eyes.
- Arm, leg, back and neck braces.
- Durable medical equipment, including wheelchairs, walkers and hospital beds.
- Diagnostic and screening tests for hearing and vision problems.
- Oxygen equipment prescribed by a doctor for home use.
- Kidney dialysis and kidney transplants. Under limited circumstances, heart and liver transplants in a Medicare-approved facility.
- Medical supplies and items such ostomy bags, surgical dressings, splints and casts.
- One pair of glasses following cataract surgery.
- Some treatment of mental illness (50% of recognized outpatient charges, unless hospital admission would have been necessary without it; then, 80% of recognized charges).
- Certain drugs that cannot be self-administered.
- Rental or purchase of durable medical equipment to be used in the home.
- There is only one chiropractic service covered. That is manipulation of the spine to correct a dislocation that can be shown by an x-ray. (Medicare does not pay for an x-ray performed by a Chiropractor.)
- Prostate cancer screenings.
- Transplants—heart, lung, liver.

Durable Medical Equipment

Wheelchairs and other durable medical equipment are covered only when prescribed by a doctor for use at home and are provided by a supplier approved by Medicare. You can find out what equipment is covered and whether a supplier is approved by calling Medicare's durable medical equipment (DME) regional carrier for your area.

This is the least regulated area in the Medicare system and the one in which a great deal of abuse occurs. Be wary of suppliers who try to get you to take equipment by telling you they will accept Medicare's 80% as their full payment and you will not have to pay anything. *Don't agree to accept equipment unless your own doctor has told you that you need it.*

- Home health services (as under Part A, but with payment by either Part A or Part B only).
- Artificial replacements for limbs, eyes, and all or part of internal body organs, including colostomy bags and supplies.
- Braces for limbs, back, or neck.
- Pneumococcal vaccination or immunizations required because of injury or risk of infection.
- Annual physical examinations and flu shots.
- Some heart, kidney, bone marrow, and liver transplants.
- Every-other-year mammograms for women 65 and over, and certain disabled women (limits by age).

NOTE: The National Cancer Institute, March 1997, joined the American Cancer Society in recommending routine mammograms for all women in their 40s. The Cancer Institute recommends testing every year or two whereas the Cancer Society has come out for annual tests. Either way, the consensus seem to hold that there is no good reason for women in their 40s to avoid these potentially life-saving screening tests to detect cancer. All groups have long recommended that women 50 and up undergo mammography. Line issue of whether mammograms are effective in younger women from 40 to 50 is difficult to evaluate. It has been recommended that individual women and their doctors make their own decisions on whether mammography is warranted.

Some Part B benefits have special requirements and some are more strictly limited than others. Pap smears, for example, are generally covered once every three years, mammograms every 24 months.

Ambulance Services

The ambulance benefit is also strictly limited. Medicare will help pay for the service only if:

1. The ambulance, equipment and personnel meet Medicare requirements and;
2. Transportation in any other vehicle could endanger your health.

Coverage is generally restricted to transportation between your home and a hospital, your home and a skilled nursing facility, or a hospital and a skilled nursing home.

SERVICES NOT COVERED BY PART B

- Services not medically necessary or reasonable and charges that exceed Medicare-approved charges.
- Eyeglasses (except after cataract surgery), dental care, hearing aids, foot care, and orthopedic shoes.
- Private-duty nursing, unless medically necessary.
- Custodial nursing home care.
- Services paid for by other government programs or workers' compensation.
- Services performed by a relative or household member.
- Cosmetic surgery, unless to correct accidental injury or to improve function of a malformation.
- Most prescription drugs and medicines taken at home.
- Screening mammography for women under 34.
- Routine physicals.

NOTE: This is a general list, and in most of these categories there are limitations imposed beyond those of approved charges. See *The Medicare Handbook* or check with your Medicare carrier for details.

BENEFITS FOR PEOPLE WITH KIDNEY FAILURE

Regardless of age, people with end-stage renal disease are often eligible for Medicare Parts A and B, including payment for kidney dialysis and costs related to kidney transplant for both beneficiaries and donors. Besides extending to Social Security and Medicare beneficiaries, spouses and dependents (children) of beneficiaries and covered workers may also be eligible for this benefit. If you or a member of your family has kidney disease, it is important to learn more about this benefit. Contact Social Security and ask that they send a booklet entitled "Medicare Coverage of Kidney Dialysis and Kidney Transplant Services."

SERVICES UNDER SPECIAL CIRCUMSTANCES

Under special circumstances, Medicare Part B will help pay for limited services by podiatrists, chiropractors, nurse practitioners, and social workers as well as for non-routine dental services related to a medical condition and lenses provided by an optometrist after cataract surgery. It may also pay for comprehensive outpatient services you receive from a rehabilitation facility and for day treatment for mental health problems.

If you do not have Part A coverage, Part B will pay for 100% of limited home healthcare, including part-time skilled nursing, physical, speech, and/or occupational therapy, medical social services, and medical supplies. Part B will also pay for 80% of medical equipment to home care.

Kidney Disease

People of all ages with end-stage renal disease (permanent kidney failure) are usually eligible for Medicare, even if they are not eligible to receive DI benefits. See section above.

Drug Addiction and Alcoholism

A new law, which became effective in March 1996, determines the way Social Security and Supplemental Security Income (SSI) disability benefits are paid to people who are disabled because of drug and/or alcohol addiction. This law applies to people who are already getting benefits, or who become newly entitled to benefits because drug addiction and/or alcoholism prevents them from working. (See the chapter on Disability Benefits for complete details.)

The SSA pays benefits under both the Disability Insurance program and SSI. Both programs pay monthly benefits to people who are so severely disabled they can't work at any job. Under the 1996 law, if your disability is based on drug addiction and/or alcoholism:

■ Your benefits must be paid to a "representative payee" (see below).
■ You must undergo and make progress in appropriate treatment for your addiction or addictions, if it is available.
■ You can receive disability benefits on the basis of your drug addiction and/or alcoholism for no more than 36 months.

Treatment Requirement

If you receive Social Security or SSI disability benefits because of drug addiction and/or alcoholism, you are required to receive treatment for your disability. The SSA will refer you to an agency that will decide what treatment is appropriate for your condition and determine if treatment is available. That agency will also verify whether you go for and make progress in available treatment.

Benefit Suspension

Payments stop if you do not participate and make progress in available treatment. Each time you stop treatment and then return, your benefits will stop for a longer period of time. For example, the first time you stop treatment and then return, your benefits stop for an additional 2 months. The second time, they stop for an additional 3 months. Each time you stop taking available treatment, the SSA will notify you the month before they stop your benefits.

Termination of Benefits

Under present law, you may receive benefits for no more than 36 months if your disability results from drug addiction and/or alcoholism. In counting the 36-month period, the SSA does not count the months when your benefits were suspended. If you are receiving disability benefits, they also do not count months when treatment was not available. The SSA sends a letter before the 36-month period ends informing you when your benefits will stop.

NOTE: When Congress enacts new welfare reform, the eligibility and payments of benefits to people with addictions is very likely to change. Check with your local Social Security office or call the toll-free number, 1-800-772-1213.

Representative Payee

Benefits paid because of drug addiction and/or alcoholism (along with some other situations and conditions) must be sent to a representative payee, who manages the money for the beneficiary. This representative payee may be a non-profit social service agency, a governmental social service agency or public guardian, another organization, or a family member the SSA approves to act in the best interest of the beneficiary.

Organizations that serve as payee for 5 or more beneficiaries who are drug addicts or alcoholics are permitted by law to charge each individual a fee for their representative payee services. The allowed monthly fee is 10% of the monthly benefit or $50, whichever is less.

CLAIM NUMBER AND MEDICARE CARD

When you become a Medicare enrollee, you will be sent a card showing what your coverage is (Parts A and B, either or both) and a number—your Social Security number plus a letter. This is your claim number, and no claim will be processed without it. Always carry your Medicare card with you; you will be asked to show it anytime you go for medical services.

NOTE: If you are in doubt about whether or not a particular service is covered, don't hesitate to call the SSA's tollfree number, your insurance intermediary, or your insurance carrier and ask.

There are some other problems that might arise, most simply due to the volume of paperwork involved.

A provider has a year within which to submit a claim to Medicare. If a claim is not submitted promptly, it may cause a problem for you if you have paid the bill yourself and are waiting for its submission to get your money back. What you can do in this situation is to call the provider, request the backup data for the claim, and offer to file it yourself. If that doesn't work, call (politely) every day until the claim is filed. Ask for a copy.

NOTE: If you are in doubt as to whether a service is covered, call your Medicare carrier. The 1-800 number can be found in your *Medicare Handbook* or provided by the telephone company 1-800 service in your area.

FILING MEDICAL INSURANCE CLAIMS

1. Read the forms carefully before you fill them out. Be sure all of the bills you are including are forms from the provider's office. These should show:
   - Name, address, and telephone number of the provider. If it is a group practice, *circle your doctor's name.*
   - Date and place of service.
   - Your name and Medicare (and/or other insurance) number.
   - Itemized and totaled charges for services performed.
   - Specific diagnosis or description of services performed—this may be a number code.
2. Do not pay bills as soon as you receive them—wait for Medicare.
3. Submit *copies* of bills unless the originals are required. If there are many bills, copy several on one page, and circle charges with a colored pen.
4. Submit your bills separately from your spouse's. A claim may include more than one service, or services performed on several dates, but there must be only one person per claim.

5. Find out whether you have to bill your Medigap policy yourself.

6. For Medigap (not Medicare) coverage that pays for prescription drugs, be sure to circle the *refill* date on the receipt. A rejection can result here if the processor sees only the original date and finds it has already been paid.

7. Mail the correct claim to the correct address.

8. Keep written records of all problems; keep all files for five years, including canceled checks.

9. Be prompt—reply to all requests for more information as soon as possible.

10. Read, process, and save your EOMB's, matching dates of services from bills with them.

11. Be sure everything that requires a signature is, in fact, signed.

WHEN A CLAIM IS REJECTED

Usually the first indication that there is a problem is when you receive the Explanation of Medicare Benefits (EOMB). The explanation offered on this form usually is enough to tell you what the problem is, but at times it isn't. You can call the carrier for a fuller explanation. Many carriers have special hot line numbers for just this purpose.

The most common reasons for rejecting claims are that the deductible has not been met, the form is not complete (usually not signed), the claim has already been paid, or there was a duplicate claim.

Some of these problems can be avoided by keeping very careful, chronological records of all medical services and then tracking all the deductibles, claims applications, and payments for each one. It also helps to have a clear understanding of what services are covered by Medicare and what services are covered by any other insurance you may have.

WHEN YOU DON'T HAVE TO PAY

Often Medicare will refuse to pay all or part of a bill, but there are times when you do not have to pay either.

You do not have to pay more than your share of the Medicare approved charges if the provider has agreed to accept assignment.

You do not have to pay for a service that Medicare does not cover unless you can reasonably have been expected to know that the service was not covered, or was not (medically) reasonable and necessary. This means you have to have been told in writing from an appropriate source that the services was not covered.

NOTE: This source could be a prior notice from your provider or insurance company, but *The Medicare Handbook* is also considered an appropriate source. If you have questions about what you should pay, contact your Medicare carrier for information and advice.

If you have difficulty finding the answers to any question you may have concerning either Part A or Part B of Medicare, the following offices can be of great help.

MEDICARE HEART DISEASE AND TRANSPLANTS

Medicare has taken giant steps to help those who are suffering from heart disease and those who require transplants.

The number of people waiting for heart transplants far exceeds the number available organs, and patients have been kept alive by the use of miraculous devices that have been developed over the last few years.

Medicare payments vary for using such devices depending on the circumstances of each case and the differences in hospitals' billing decisions and payment scales in the various states.

These devices that maintain life while patients await donated organs are now part of healthcare available as a bridge to transplants.

The Health Care Financing Administration (HCFA) has approved to date three models: Thermo Cardio Systems, Aviomed and Thoratec, as such bridges and has indicated that in the near future other models will be approved from time to time. These approvals occurred in 1996 and the Medicare program

Health Care Financing Administration Regional Offices		
Customer Services	Regional Office	States Served
617-565-1232	Boston	CT, ME, MA, NJ, RI, VT
212-264-3657	New York	NY, NJ, PR, VI
215-596-1332	Philadelphia	DE, DC, MD, PA, VA, WV
404-331-2044	Atlanta	AL, FL, GA, KY, MS, NC, SC, TN
312-353-7180	Chicago	IL, IN, MI, MN, OH, WI
214-767-6401	Dallas	AR, LA, NM, OK, TX
816-426-2866	Kansas City	IA, KS, MO, NE
303-844-4024	Denver	CO, MT, ND, SD, UT
415-744-3602	San Francisco	AZ, CA, GU, HI, NV
206-615-2354	Seattle	AK, ID, OR, WA
TTY For the Hearing and Speech Impaired: 1-800-820-1202		

for the elderly and disabled have been paying for such use.

The patient must however establish by substantial evidence the need for a new heart. By using such machines, the patient can move up on the waiting list for a donor heart. Medicare will pay about $15,000 for a patient to be on such devices as well as about $3,000 for surgeon's fees associated with installing and removing such devices.

Heart transplants are quite expensive, usually about $100,000 and the annual cost to Medicare over the past few years has been approximately $45,000,000, reflecting only the costs associated with the procedure and immediate postoperative care, without considering associated drug expenses.

The ground rules set by HCFA require that the patient be approved and listed as a candidate by a Medicare heart transplant center. Such centers are located in your community. The United Network for Organ Sharing keeps current records on transplant data.

HCFA requires surgeons to make every reasonable effort to transplant patients on such devices as soon as practicable.

Heart transplant operations require many extremely complicated procedures, resources, talent and supervision. Each year more than 900,000 American die of heart disease, and reports indicate that it is the number-one killer for both sexes.

Many patients are saved by new clot-busting drugs, improved cardiology techniques and open-heart surgery. Total expenditures for treatments of heart disease amount to approximately $115 billion per year.

For HMOs, the expense is a major problem and all of them would like to keep such costs under control. As a result, some HMOs have limited tests and surgeries for some people with heart disease and perform heart surgery about half as often as the national average. Many seek the lowest cost and negotiate rock-bottom contracts for such services. While such procedures do not necessarily mean that patients are receiving less than expert care, it would seem appropriate that patients needing such care should check out "centers of excellence" for heart disease treatments and organ transplants.

Coronary-artery bypass surgery (CABS), once a radical feat, has become standardized, high-volume procedure. You might reach the conclusion that if one hospital or another has better prices and does a high volume that their operating teams are more efficient and talented and should therefore be selected by the patient.

However price and volume should not be the only determining factor in selecting the hospital or service. The patient should investigate hospitals on the basis of patient survival ratio instead of volume or price. It may mean the difference between life and death. The patient should ask the cardiologist of choice to provide a list of hospitals specializing in heart disease and CABS procedures with respective mortality rates. Over the past few years, reports have indicated that some hospitals have had between 1.4% and 3% mortality rates.

Mortality rate data has been available since the early 1990s, adjusted for factors like patients' age and medical complications, so that hospitals handling many difficult cases can be compared against hospitals with easier cases. Dr. Mark Chassen of New York has been a compiler of such data since 1990 and some hospitals and surgeons use his findings to identify problems and improve performance.

In cases involving children, traditionally the Medicaid programs of most states allow gravely ill children to use whatever doctor, surgeon or hospital is selected by the parents. Financial aspects of this choice are very important but it is more essential to obtain the top talent and services particularly in the first few weeks of a child's life. This is no time to shop around for the best price. Just get the best talent for the benefit of the patient whether a child or adult.

UPDATE

All Medicare beneficiaries must be alert to the changes that are taking place in healthcare policies.

The *New York Times* reported that Medicare beneficiaries will soon receive information about health insurance options to give beneficiaries a wider variety of choices like those available to many workers in private industry who are covered by employer plans.

The government plans an extensive education and publicity campaign and will soon send a new Medicare handbook, with a detailed description of all the options, to every Medicare beneficiary's household.

The new options, most of which will become available late this year, offer possible extra benefits, including prescription drugs and other items not covered by the standard Medicare program. But they may also expose beneficiaries to higher costs and more uncertainty.

Different options will be available in different parts of the country, and no one knows for sure how many private health plans will enter the potentially lucrative Medicare market. If beneficiaries are satisfied with the way they get healthcare now, they do not have to make a change.

In the light of this report everyone who has a question about any plan should ask for answers to all questions or benefits, limitations, and beneficiary costs before adopting the plan being presented for approval.

Most important of all, ask if you can make a change to a new plan if you are dissatisfied and what time limitations there may be if you change your mind.

Medicare Part A Summary
Hospital Insurance—Covered Services Per Benefit Period

Service	Benefit	Medicare Pays	You Pay
Hospitalization			
Semiprivate room and board, general nursing, miscellaneous hospital services and supplies	First 60 days 61st to 90th day 91st to 150th day Beyond 150 days	All but $768 All but $192 All but $384 Nothing	$768 $192 $384 All costs
Post-Hospital Skilled Nursing Facility Care			
You must have been in a hospital for at least 3 days and the facility within 30 days after hospital discharge	First 20 days Additional 80 days Beyond 100 days	100% of approved amount All but $96.00/day Nothing	Nothing $96.00/day All costs
Home Health Care	Part-time or intermittent care for as long as you meet Medicare requirements	100% of approved services, 80% of approved amount for durable medical equipment	Nothing for services, 20% approved amount for durable medical equipment
Hospice Care	As long as doctor certifies need	All, but limits on costs for outpatient drugs and inpatient respite care	Limited cost for outpatient drugs and respite care
Blood	Unlimited if medically necessary	All but first three pints per calendar year	For first three pints (or replace)

Benefit period begins 1st hospital day, ends 60 days after release from facility.
Facility must be approved by Medicare.
Reserve days (60), nonrenewable.
Neither Medicare nor Medigap will pay for custodial care; you must pay for such care or buy special insurance.
Blood deductible for a calendar year may be met under either A or B.
These figures are for 1999 and are subject to change.

Medicare Part B Summary
Medical Insurance—Covered Services Per Benefit Period

Service	Benefit	Medicare Pays	You Pay
Medical Expenses			
Doctors' services, inpatient and outpatient medical and surgical supplies, physical speech therapy, ambulance, diagnostic tests, and more	Medicare pays for medical services in or out of the hospital	80% of approved amount after $100 deductible	$100 deductible plus 20% of approved amount and limited charges above
Clinical Laboratory Services			
Blood tests, biopsies, urinalyses, and more	Unlimited if medically necessary	100% of approved amounts	Nothing for services
Home Health Care			
Medically necessary skilled care	Part-time or intermittent skilled care for as long as you meet conditions for benefits	100% of approved amounts, 80% of approved amount for durable medical equipment	Nothing for services, 20% of approved amount for durable medical equipment
Outpatient Hospital Treatment			
Services for the diagnosis or treatment of illness or injury	Unlimited if medically necessary	80% of approved amount after $100 deductible	$100 deductible plus 20% of billed charges
Blood	Unlimited if medically necessary	80% of approved amount after $100 deductible and starting with 4th pint	First three pints plus 20% of approved amount for additional pints after $100 deductible

Once you have had $100 of expenses for covered services in 1999 the Part B deductible does not apply to any further services you receive for the rest of the year. **These figures are for 1999 and are subject to change.**

CHAPTER FOUR

Travel Outside the United States: Your Healthcare

The reader should be aware that Medicare does not cover healthcare costs outside the United States except under limited circumstances in Canada and Mexico.

If you intend to travel overseas, coverage should be considered for the following:

1. Direct payment to hospitals and doctors instead of reimbursement of expenses after the fact.
2. Ambulance expense coverage.
3. Emergency transportation back to the U.S.
4. Loss of medication or glasses.
5. Accidental death.
6. Trip cancellation losses.
7. Lost luggage.

There are a number of types of policies and coverage and fine print must be read carefully. Some of the points to look for are:

■ The maximum that will be paid for medical expenses, including hospital and doctor's bills, ambulance costs, medications and transportation.
■ Whether the plan provides for toll-free assistance to help you find local medical care, contact with doctors in the U.S. and arrangement for emergency transportation to the U.S. or elsewhere.
■ Whether coverage is excluded for pre-existing ailments or conditions for which a doctor was consulted or that required treatment or medication for any

set period prior to the effective date of the policy. (Some policies exclusion period is 60 days, some 90 days and some 180 days.)
■ Most policies provide that the insurer is only "secondarily liable" to the extent-of expenses not covered in your regular health insurance. (You might want to check with your agent to find out what coverage you do have and then ask for recommendations of policies to cover gaps in your U.S. coverage.)

NOTE: Currently of the ten Medigap policies authorized to be issued, A & B do not cover overseas medical or hospital expenses. C to J include some coverage. (The National Council of Senior Citizens 1-800-596-6272 and AARP 1-800-523-5800 can supply details of such plans for your information.) See chart page 59.

Family Medical Leave Act

The Family Medical Leave Act became effective in August 1993 and was hailed by all as a breakthrough in United States family policy. It mandates 12 weeks of unpaid, job-guaranteed leave for childbirth, adoption or illness of an employee or family member but applies only to businesses with 50 or more employees.

Many employers have not posted notices informing employees of their family leave rights as required by law and a number of surveys since the passage of the Act have indicated that compliance by employers has not been initiated either because of ignorance of the law or lack of attention.

Many companies err in assuming that because they already allow some kind of medical or childbirth leave they are in compliance with the federal law. In fact, the law requires significant changes in even liberal policies. Unlike most employer policies that give the employee some control, the current law in most cases denies supervisors any discretion in granting leave. The law also allows the employee to take such leave in portions of a few hours or a few days at a time.

The confusion in interpreting the law has deterred many employees from exercising such rights and in cases where the leave had to be taken by the employee some have lost their jobs and have had to appeal to the labor department charged with implementing the law.

Many employees are having problems in arranging leave with employers. The University of California and a number of offices of the National Association of Working Women in the various states have surveyed the problem and have found that approximately 50% of employers have not posted notices informing employees of their family leave rights as required by the law and were failing to allow 12 weeks leave, to guarantee jobs, or to continue benefits during leave. The surveys also indicated that about 60% of those who took leave had problems with their employers.

Until industry has had time to realize that the law exists and will be enforced, employees will have to work out such leave problems as they have in the past.

Many employers feel that such "family leave" only applies to a woman who has a child and wants family leave to care for the child, and ignores many situations where a wife becomes ill and the husband (employee) requires leave to care for his wife and children which is covered by the application for leave "for illnesses of the family or required assistance for members of the employee's family."

Employees should contact the Human Resources Department or the executive in charge of personnel relations to determine whether the company is aware of the Family Leave Act and its policies with respect to compliance before taking such "leave."

CHAPTER SIX
Hospices and Custodial Care

HOSPICES

Hospice care should not be confused with custodial care. A hospice is a program designed to make sure that the final chapter of a dying person's life takes place among family and friends, in the home or in a homelike setting.

The intent is to eliminate the hospital bright lights, noises, sterile surroundings, machines and general activities of the hospital.

There are about 2,000 hospice programs in the United States, providing doctors, nurses, counselors and other health professionals to help a dying patient remain comfortable.

Hospice teams may also provide nursing and home health support. Most hospice programs require only that the person have a limited life expectancy of 6 months and a letter from the attending physician to that effect.

The National Hospice Organization (1-800-658-8898) can provide a guide to the nation's hospices.

Hospice benefits may be received in lieu of standard Medicare benefits while retaining Medicare coverage for all other illnesses or injuries.

CUSTODIAL CARE

Custodial care is defined as assistance that does not require medical or paramedical training. It consists of help with the activities of daily living, bathing, dressing, eating, getting in and out of bed, walking, taking medication, going to the bathroom and the like.

Such care is not covered by Medicare, with the exception of hospice care.

Services covered by Medicare and services that are not covered are set forth in the chapter dealing with Medicare.

The Census Bureau estimates that by the year 2040, approximately 76 million Americans will be 65 and older, 13 million will be over 85 and about 6 million disabled will be cared for at home by one or more members of the family.

At the present time, the Census Bureau reports that there are 1.6 million men and women being cared for in nursing homes at a cost of $49 billion per year with approximately $25 billion being paid for by Medicaid.

When the family decides that it needs additional help to meet the needs of an aging or disabled member of the family, the services of different sources will probably be required. Finding such sources that can provide home care services usually follows this procedure—discussions with friends or relatives that have had home care experience, your family doctor who may have worked with home care agencies or have other patients who have had good results with particular providers of such care, the social service director or administrator of your local hospital who can refer the family to qualified home care agencies, the local chapter of visiting nurses association will have lists of visiting nurses or practical nurses or aides, and local community groups including religious and fraternal organizations of senior citizen centers usually have a list of home care providers who have made their names available for such services.

In addition to the decision to have a home care provider in the home, there is also the possibility that such expense may be reduced by investigating the availability of an adult care center (ADC) in your area. A recent estimate of adult care centers in the United States is about 3,000 and growing. This service has been found to be a less expensive alternative to nursing home care and may be more acceptable to the person requiring such care than residence in a nursing home, and more important, the person utilizing ADC can remain at home and avoid nursing home costs that may be expensive while a day in ADC may run approximately $20 to $80 per day.

ADC facilities vary materially. Many seek to alleviate feelings of isolation or loneliness by providing recreational activities such as singing, dancing, painting and the like, while others provide medical services in addition to other services. Finding an appropriate ADC can be accomplished by contacting your local Agency on Aging or by calling the National Institute on Adult Day Care, National Coalition on Aging (NCOA), 409 Third Street, S.W., Washington, D.C. 20024 (202-619-0724). The reader should be aware that ADC fees may range from $20 to $80 a day. However, these fees are not covered by Medicare or by private insurance. If the patient requires a wheelchair, walker or other equipment for treatment or rehabilitation the family might save some money by checking with the local Red Cross or Salvation Army office, or call the AOA 800-number set forth in the text.

Another alternative that may be considered is the employment of a geriatric care manager who is a professional counselor able to assess the healthcare assistance that the patient may require and the most efficient way financially to obtain such care, as well as finding proper and acceptable home care services. Information of such managers can be obtained from The National Association of Private Geriatric Care Managers (601-881-8008).

Before deciding upon a manager, the family should review the following: The manager's educational background? How long in business—full-time or part-time? Does the manager have a license to perform such services? What references does the manager have from other families that have been served? (Check them out by talking to the people or family served.) What is the manager's availability? Is it a one-person practice? What happens when the manager goes on vacation: How is the patient covered? What are the total specific fees charged for the services? And, get a list of the services that are provided. Get everything in writing and be sure the family is clear on all points. Do not hesitate to ask and get answers to all of the questions you may have.

If the family cannot afford the healthcare that is required, determine what expenses are covered under Medicaid. See chapter on Medicaid.

If nursing home care is required, be aware that the aging, disabled or patient requiring long-term care might be able to qualify for Medicaid which does cover nursing home care.

Another source of information would be Children of Aging Parents (CAP), Levittown, PA 19057 (215-345-5104) that offers publications on care for the elderly and Office of Technical Assessment, U.S. Government Printing Office, Washington, D.C. 20402 (202-783-3238) for publications relating to scientific information on progress being made with respect to specific illnesses.

CHAPTER SEVEN
What Every Patient Should Know

DIAGNOSIS-RELATED GROUPS

Every patient should be aware of how they are billed by hospitals for the treatment of diagnosed illness or injuries.

Diagnosis-Related Groups (DRG) is a coding system based on 500 groups that encompass more than 3,500 medical procedures and 12,514 diagnostic codes. A predetermined standard rate, or average cost, for particular categories of treatment is set for each type of case as identified in the DRG list. The list also specifies the length of hospital stay for the determined condition. These determinations and allocated cost for treatment were originally reviewed by PROs but for the past few years such reviews were reduced or eliminated by the government in favor of a substitute reliance for accuracy of determination left to a few entities to conduct a smaller number of more sophisticated computer-based reviews.

Many hospitals discovered that under this form of supervision it became easy to "upcode" the determination of treatment and bill for the highest amount available. Few of the millions of bills filed each year are scrutinized and the higher bills are paid.

An example of how "upcodes" might work are the following: Real Condition DRG Code 143–Chest Pain-reimbursement $2,089. Upcoded condition to DRG Code 129–Cardiac Condition, Unexplained-reimbursement $4,526.

The impact on the patient's pocketbook is clear. If Medicare-approved payment is $16,726 and paid 80% of the bill, i.e., $13,380, the patient's 20% would be $3,346.

Hospital billings using upcoded determinations are the focus of investigators from the Department of Health and Human Services (HHS) Office of Inspector general.

The New York-based regional inspector general for HHS has issued a warning to hospitals. "Don't upcode—bill for what you do and do what you bill for." HHS has currently targeted hospital fraud as a major area of inquiry.

News coverage indicates that while managed care has reduced healthcare inflation by about 3% a year, Medicare costs are growing at three times such rate and the problem of upcoding seems to affect the operations of both for-profit and not-for-profit hospitals.

What can a patient do? The patient can ask the doctor or hospital what the "code" determination of the particular illness or treatment is and what the fee is related to such code? If the patient has the recommended treatment and after a review of the bill feels that it is too high, the patient can discuss the services and related bill with the doctor or the hospital. If the result of such discussion is not satisfactory to the patient the patient can file a complaint with the Office of the Inspector General of HHS before paying any part of the bill not covered by his or her health plan or insurance. Provide the Inspector General with all of the details of the diagnosis and treatment and let the government decide what the healthcare services were and what should be paid by the patient. If this procedure does not result in a decision acceptable to the patient, the patient can seek legal advice and go to court to reduce the bill.

Medigap Insurance: Do You Need It?

MEDIGAP INSURANCE

Many people have, or will want to have, other insurance to pay for things Medicare does not cover. Some people are covered by a group plan (such as an HMO), their employer's health plan either as a worker or retiree, or as the spouse of a worker or retiree.

Medicare considers such plans to be primary payers, with Medicare as a secondary payer. With new data-sharing capabilities, Medicare can now check to see if you are covered by such a plan.

Employment-related plans can be quite comprehensive and frequently offer enough benefits to round out Medicare coverage. Even if you have to pay some of the premium, it is often a bargain. The best thing to do is have a clear understanding of what both the employer and Medicare plans cover, and then check to see if anything important to you is left uncovered.

Many people buy extra insurance to cover Medicare's deductible and coinsurance costs and to pick up some of the other non-payable charges medical care can generate. This coverage is called "Medigap" insurance, and it comes in many forms. So many different policies were developed, and confusion and abuse were so prevalent, that Congress passed a law standardizing this coverage and governing its sale.

There are now 10 packages of Medigap insurance, offering everything from a basic plan with limited coverage through a comprehensive policy. Insurers can sell these policies—and only these policies—as Medigap insurance. (Schedule Annexed).

All companies must offer the most basic policy, though they don't have to carry the others, and not all plans may be available in all states.

The plans (identified with a letter, "A" for the simplest through "J" for the most comprehensive) are all the same, regardless of which company offers them, but the premiums for the same policy may vary from company to company or in different areas of the country. Of course, the more coverage you want, the higher premium you will pay, regardless of where you buy it.

NOTE: New Medicare enrollees, ages 65 or older, cannot be rejected for Medigap insurance if they sign up for it within 6 months of enrolling in Medicare. This is a new law; before, Medigap insurers were free to reject applicants for health reasons.

Any Medigap policy must offer the following basic benefits:

- Payment of the patient's share of Medicare approved amounts for physician services (usually 20%) after the patient meets the $100 annual Part B deductible.

- Payment of Medicare's Part A coinsurance charges for long hospital stays up to a lifetime total of 365 days of inpatient hospital coverage.

You will see that *none* of these plans covers extended nursing home care or home care for chronic conditions such as Alzheimer's disease. You may want to look into another policy for long-term care. Be aware, however, that this is an area which has not yet been standardized by government regulation, though it may be in the near future.

You may not need one of these new policies if you already have Medigap coverage that includes amenities such as private rooms and private-duty nurses. These are benefits the new policies don't cover.

If you are receiving Medicaid, you don't need a Medigap policy—Medicaid covers it all.

Law forbids the sale of more than one Medigap policy to a person, and there is a $25,000 fine for doing so.

If you are new to the Medigap market, decide what coverage you need and do some comparison shopping. It bears repeating that Medicare and Medigap policies do not provide much protection for long-term care, and you may want to consider some sort of nursing home custodial coverage policy. The current turmoil in the insurance industry suggests that it would be prudent to buy your policy from a well-established, reputable company.

ANOTHER ALTERNATIVE: PREPAID HEALTHCARE PLANS

In response to rising healthcare costs, Health Maintenance Organizations (HMOs) and other forms of managed healthcare offering medical services on a prepayment basis have come into being. By charging a monthly fee to people who enroll, these plans can provide, theoretically, a number of treatment and diagnostic services for less money than would be charged on a per-case or per-visit basis.

Services provided by these umbrella organizations include those covered under both Part A and Part B of Medicare, with some plans providing services Medicare doesn't cover at all, such as prescription drugs.

If you are a Medicare beneficiary, you may enroll in a prepaid healthcare plan, but you must be sure that it is Medicare-eligible.

If the plan is eligible, you are entitled to receive all the services and supplies to which you are entitled under Medicare coverage. Medicare makes direct payments to the organization for the services it provides.

In addition to a set monthly prepayment for services in one of these plans, you may also be required to pay a deductible and any coinsurance you would have been expected to pay for equivalent Medicare services if you were not enrolled.

NOTE: Since there may be several prepayment plans in your area, you will need to do some comparison shopping to find out what each offers and what combination of services best meets your needs. Look in the classified section of your local telephone directory under "Health Maintenance Organizations."

For additional information, see chapter on HMOs and Managed Care Services.

Medigap Insurance Benefits Summary

The National Association of Insurance Commissioners has developed 10 standard Medigap policies to simplify supplementary health insurance offerings for Medicare beneficiaries. Insurance companies supplying medigap policies do not have to offer all 10 plans, but all companies must offer Policy A, and all plans must offer the basic benefits described in detail on page TK

Coverage	A	B	C	D	E	F	G	H	I	J
Basic benefits	×	×	×	×	×	×	×	×	×	×
Skilled nursing coinsurance			×	×	×	×	×	×	×	×
Part A deductible		×	×	×	×	×	×	×	×	×
Part B deductible			×			×				×
Part B excess 100%						×			×	×
Part B excess 80%							×			
Foreign travel emergency			×	×	×	×	×	×	×	×
At-home recovery				×			×		×	×
Basic drugs $1,250 limit								×	×	
Extended drugs $3,000 limit										×
Preventive Care					×					×
Estimated yearly premium*	$400-600	$500-700	$500-700	$500-800	$550-850	$650-900	$600-700	$700-900	$850-1,400	$1,200-1,800

Varies widely from state to state

10 Standard Medigap Plans	
Plan	**Coverage**
A	Covers basic benefits, including the daily co-payment for hospital days 61–90 per benefit period, the higher daily co-payment for hospital days 91–150, and the full cost of 365 additional hospital days per lifetime.
B	Pays basic benefits plus the Part A deductible
C	Like Plan B, but includes the Part B deductible. It includes a daily co-payment for days 21–100 in a skilled nursing home and covers foreign emergency care.
D	Like Plan C, but excludes the Part B deductible and includes short-term home health care.
E	Like Plan D, but excludes home care and includes preventive health screening.
F	Like Plan C, and pays for all doctor fees not covered by Medicare.
G	Like Plan D, and pays for 80 percent of doctor fees not covered.
H	Like Plan D, but excludes home care and includes limited coverage for prescription drugs.
I	Like plan G, but includes 100 percent of doctor fees not covered by Medicare and limited coverage for prescription drugs.
J	Covers everything above, plus prescription drugs.

CHAPTER NINE

Health Directives and Living Wills

ADVANCE HEALTH CARE DIRECTIVES

All adult patients admitted to a hospital or nursing home, or receiving medical attention from a home health agency or treatment covered by Medicare or Medicaid, must be informed of their options with respect to life-sustaining treatment. This includes the option of a Living Will. These patients also must be given a description of the current state law governing these situations and the hospital's own internal policies on patients' rights. For this reason, most doctors, as well as hospitals and nursing homes, now have forms they give out routinely.

There are two basic kinds of documents, known as advance directives, that outline a patient's wishes for treatment: Durable Powers Of Attorney and Living Wills. They are not the same.

A Durable Power of Attorney for Health Care is a document which names a person and an alternate to make healthcare decisions for you should you not be able to do it yourself. It can also tell, either in a general manner or in specific ways, how you wish to be cared for so that anyone named to act on your behalf will have your guidance.

A Living Will is a document intended to give your physician information and general instructions about how you want to be treated. If you have strong feelings about specific treatments, in most states you are free to go into detail about which ones you would prefer not be used.

Whatever the document you decide upon, your doctor should have a copy on file as part of your medical record, and your family should know where a copy can be located.

It's a good idea to execute documents such as these before, or early in the course of, an illness. Even more than a durable power of attorney, having a living will means that you—rather than a member of your family, the state, or a medical committee—take the responsibility for deciding if extraordinary means should be employed in your medical treatment. Extraordinary means could include cardiac resuscitation, mechanical respiration, or artificial nutrition and hydration, and a number of other procedures you may or may not want.

If you are mentally competent, you have the right—in principle at least—to refuse to continue treatment; the right to refuse to begin treatment is better established. But if you are not mentally competent, or not conscious, recent court decisions suggest that the wishes you expressed when you were should be respected. More than 40 states now have laws recognizing living wills, and the remaining states have similar laws under review. In the meantime, if you want to address this question for yourself and your family, consult an attorney or legal aid service and arrange to provide legal means to express your wishes. It is wise to have legal advice because the laws governing this differ greatly from state to state. An attorney can help you to provide for the changes in your document that might be required because of either new medical technology or new laws.

You can get more information on your state's advance directives for healthcare by

contacting your state Attorney General's
Office or the Society for the Right to Die, 250
West 57th Street, New York, NY 10107,
212-366-5540.

CHAPTER TEN
Supplemental Security Income

SUPPLEMENTAL SECURITY INCOME

Supplemental Security Income (SSI) is a program administered through the Social Security Administration (SSA) that pays a monthly benefit to people who are in severe financial need, have little or no income, extremely limited resources, are 65 or older, or who regardless of age are blind or disabled.

ELIGIBILITY

In order to receive SSI benefits, you must meet age, disability and financial need requirements.

1. *Age.* You must be 65 years of age or older.
2. *Disability.* To meet the disability requirement you must be "blind" or "severely disabled."
3. *Financial Need.* To meet the requirement of financial need, your "resources" and "income" may not exceed the limits hereinafter set forth.

"Blindness" is defined as no better than 20/200 vision in the better eye or limited field of vision of 20 degrees or less with corrective lenses.

"Severely disabled" is based on a determination that "substantial gainful activity" is not possible because of an emotionally or physically disabling condition which is expected to last at least 12 months or result in death. This decision will be made by SSA.

Eligibility based on the disability of a child under 18 is defined as "a medically determinable impairment" which results in marked or severe functional limitations which can be expected to last for a continuous period of not less than 12 months. Previous definitions of a child's disability were eliminated from the law. An extended discussion of this status is contained elsewhere in this chapter.

Financial need is determined by a review of the applicant's "resources" and "income." Some "resources" and "income" are included in this determination, others are not considered.

To be eligible for SSI benefits in 2000, the applicant must have countable resources of less than $2,000, if married the combined resources of both parties must be less than $3,000.

Resources include any assets or things you own that can be converted into cash, such as land, securities, jewelry and other valuables.

Even if you think you may not qualify for this program, look over the lists of income and resources, particularly those items that are not counted as resources—you may be eligible.

Not Counted As Resources

■ A home that you own and its land that you use as your main living place, regardless of value.
■ Personal property or household goods with a total equity value of $2,000 are not counted; equity value in excess of $2,000 is counted. (Equity value is the amount you can sell an item for, less the amount of any legal debt against it.)

For a car, only the amount of market value in excess of $4,500 is counted; the value of a single car is not counted at all if it is used by the household for special purposes—transportation to a job, transportation to a place of regular treatment for a specific medical problem, or used for a handicapped person. If you own other cars, the equity value of each is counted.

Life insurance policies having a face value of $1,500 or less per person.

Any resources or things needed by a blind or disabled person for an approved self-support program.

Up to $1,500 in burial funds for a person and up to $1,500 in burial funds for a spouse; a burial plot for you and members of your immediate family is also not counted.

Income-producing property, regardless of value, used in a trade or business (tool of a tradesperson, machinery and livestock of a farmer) essential to self-support.

Retroactive Social Security or SSI payments are not counted as assets for 6 months after they are received.

Income held under the Uniform Gift For Minors Act or in Trust

Items Counted As Resources

Real estate (land or buildings).

Personal property and household goods (furniture, jewelry, books, appliances, etc.)

Securities (stocks and bonds).

Bank accounts (checking and savings)

The resources of an applicant's ineligible spouse or parent(s) may also be considered in determining SSI eligibility and payments, but not necessarily dollar for dollar.

In some cases, the law does not count the resources or assets of the parents of a disabled child who lives at home when determining eligibility for SSI and related Medicaid benefits. This may occur when home care of a disabled child under age 18 is a less expensive alternative than the care that would have to be provided if the child were in an institution. In other words, by disregarding the assets and income of the parents, the child may be eligible for limited SSI benefits.

If you have a young child with a severe disability, you should contact your local Social Security office to learn about this and other SSI provisions that affect disabled children and their families.

If your counted resources exceed the limits listed above, you may still be eligible for SSI. But in order to keep your eligibility for payments, you may be required to sell excess resources at fair market value within 9 months for real estate and 3 months for personal property. (Under certain conditions, excess real estate can be excluded if it cannot be sold.)

Benefits from SSI you receive while you are selling excess resources may have to be repaid to SSI after you get the sales proceeds. If you refuse to sell excess resources, you will be declared ineligible for benefits and must reimburse SSI for all payments so far received.

Income

An individual with less than $500 in unearned income in 1999 will generally qualify for SSI benefits and a couple with less than $750.

If a couple is separated for 6 months or more, then each individual is regarded as a single individual in determining income restrictions. The figures referred to herein are federal figures and do not reflect any income exclusions or payments made by state programs. Those who live in a state that supplements SSI benefits may be able to qualify for SSI benefits with more income.

Income, generally, is defined as earned or unearned, depending on the source, but assistance or compensation in lieu of (instead of) money may also be considered as income.

As with resources, some items count as income and some do not in determining eligibility for SSI.

Items Counted As Income

Money, which includes cash and checks.

Food, shelter, and clothing which are provided as compensation in lieu of money.

Earned income from sources such as wages, net earnings from self-employment, and income from sheltered workshops.

Unearned income from sources such as Social Security benefits, workers' compensation, veterans' benefits, pensions, alimony, annuities, gifts, interest, dividends, and rents.

Royalties and honorariums even if received for past work.

Items Not Counted As Income

$20 per month of earned or unearned income (except some types of unearned income based on need, such as certain veterans' pensions).

$65 per month of earned income plus one-half of earned income over $65 a month, or, if there is no unearned income, $85 a month of earned income plus one-half of the remainder over $85 a month.

Government refunds of taxes paid on real property or on food purchases.

Assistance based on need from a state or local political subdivision or Native American tribe; most federal judgment distribution payments and per capita payments of funds held in trust by the Secretary of the Interior which are made to members of Native American tribes, including purchases made with these payments.

Amounts for tuition and fees paid from grants, scholarships, and fellowships.

Medical care and services (including reimbursements and payment of health insurance premiums).

Homegrown produce consumed by the household.

Irregular or infrequent earned income totaling no more than $10 a month; irregular or infrequent unearned income totaling no more than $20 a month.

Foster care payments for a child who is not receiving SSI payments but has been placed in the recipient's household by an approved agency.

■ If a child, one-third of any child support payments received from the absent parent.

■ A limited amount of the earnings of an unmarried blind or disabled child who is a student under the age of 22.

■ If disabled or blind, the amount of income necessary for fulfillment of an approved Plan for Achieving Self-Support (PASS program); if blind, an amount equal to work expenses and if disabled an amount equal to impairment-related work expenses.

■ Food stamp assistance.

■ Housing assistance from federal housing programs run by state and local subdivisions.

■ Relocation expense assistance provided because of property acquisition for federal or federally assisted projects or by state or local governments.

■ Grants or loans to undergraduate students from the Department of Education's educational programs.

■ Assistance furnished in connection with a presidentially declared disaster and any interest earned on the assistance for the first 9 months.

■ Interest which is paid on excluded burial funds and left to accumulate.

■ Food, clothing, or shelter in a nonprofit retirement home or similar institution that is provided or paid for by a nonprofit organization which is not expressly obligated to do so.

■ Food, clothing, shelter, and home energy assistance provided in kind by a private nonprofit organization if the assistance is based on need and is certified by the state; home energy assistance provided by certain home energy suppliers if the assistance is based on need and is certified by the state.

■ Money received by a victim of a crime (excluded from resources for 9 months after the month in which payments are received if it can be shown they are compensation for expenses or losses that resulted from the crime); reparations payments to Holocaust survivors from the Federal Republic of Germany.

■ Impairment-related work expenses.

■ Federal income tax refunds related to earned income tax credits excluded from income in the month they are received and excluded from resources the following month in order to allow time for the refunds to be used.

POVERTY GUIDELINES

In many documents relating to Medicaid, Supplemental Security Income and other welfare benefits for the poor, the reader will find references to "persons below the Poverty Line."

The Department of Health and Human Services (HHS) issues poverty guidelines for administrative purposes. The guidelines are used to determine the financial eligibility criteria for a number of federal government programs.

The statistical poverty levels consist of a set of thresholds that vary by family size and composition and is a statistical measure based on income-food expenditure patterns from the Department of Agriculture Surveys of household food consumption and the cost of the minimum price of a nutritionally adequate "American style" diet (known as the Economy Food Plan.) The poverty levels are adjusted to reflect changes in the annual average Consumer Price Index (CPI).

The poverty guidelines vary by family size. They are used for determining whether a person or family is financially eligible for assistance of services under a particular federal program.

Once each year in March, a survey is made of each family in the Current Population Survey (CPS) to determine the approximate poverty threshold for the average family based on the total income of each family. If the family's total income is less than the cut-off figure the family is classified as being below the "poverty level." The official poverty threshold is computed by increasing the weighted average poverty thresholds of the preceding year by the percentage change in the CPI rounding the value for a family of four (4) to the next

higher $50. All families above and below, four (4) are computed by adding or subtracting equal dollar amounts derived from the average differences between poverty lines for families with one to eight persons rounded to the nearest multiple of $20.

Because of the complexity in determining the poverty level, the reader is advised to call the local Social Security Office or Medicaid Office for the current "poverty level" for families of two (2) or more.

Special Situations Affecting SSI Recipients of Benefits

■ Having a permanent place to live is not a requirement for receiving SSI benefits. An organization can receive SSI checks and information from SSA for homeless people. Aged, blind, and disabled residents of public shelters for the homeless (as defined by SSA regulations) may be eligible for SSI benefits for as many as 6 months in a 9-month period. Benefits for homeless people in emergency shelters will provide some income to help meet the expenses of seeking a permanent residence.

■ A needy aged, blind, or disabled person or a needy family may receive assistance from a private, nonprofit charitable organization without causing a reduction in the recipient's SSI benefits.

■ Your local SSA office can suggest state and local sources that provide social services to SSI recipients.

■ Homemaker/home healthcare services help the aged, the blind, and the disabled with their personal care, chores, and money management. Through public and private home care services, people who are having difficulty caring for themselves can be helped and continue to live independently in their own homes. These services may also provide assistance in making new living arrangements in residential or family care facilities. Visiting volunteers and special help for people with disabilities are other services available.

For those receiving SSI disability benefits, special rules make it possible to receive SSI, Medicare, or Medicaid while holding a job. (Similar rules also apply to those receiving Social Security Disability Insurance benefits) In fact, the Social Security Administration encourages people to be independent and helps them to prepare themselves to work.

If you are an SSI beneficiary interested in working, or preparing yourself to go to work, you should see the work incentives specialist at your local Social Security office for more information about the programs.

Disabled or blind SSI recipients who work may continue to receive payments until countable income exceeds SSI limits. Medicaid may continue for disabled or blind SSI recipients who earn over the SSI limits if the person cannot afford similar medical care and depends on Medicaid in order to work.

If a person recovers while participating in a vocational rehabilitation program and is likely to become self-supporting, benefits may continue until the program ends.

Pay received in a sheltered workshop is treated as earned income, whether or not it is considered wages for other purposes. This enables Social Security to exclude more earnings of a sheltered workshop employee when computing his or her SSI payment.

Deductions for Work Expenses

If you are disabled, certain impairment-related work expenses can be deducted from earned income, but the SSA must approve each deduction and the amount. The following work expenses generally are deductible:

Wheelchairs, respirators, braces, and other medical devices.

Attendant care services, such as assistance in going to and from work, a reader for the blind, or an interpreter for the deaf.

Transportation costs that are extraordinary, such as modifications to a vehicle.

■ One-handed typewriters, braille devices, telecommunications devices for the deaf, and certain other work-related equipment.
■ Regularly prescribed drugs and medical services needed to control an impairment.
■ Residential modifications, such as ramps or railings outside the home that improve mobility.
■ Expendable medical supplies, costs of keeping a guide dog, and other miscellaneous expenses.

Blind recipients are allowed deductions for certain work expenses in addition to those mentioned above. Examples are federal, state, and Social Security taxes, routine transportation costs to and from work, and union dues. These work expenses will not be counted in determining a blind recipient's eligibility or SSI payment amount.

To assure that blind beneficiaries learn about any changes that may affect their monthly payments, Social Security will either telephone them or send their notices by certified mail if they request this service.

Provisions relating to persons receiving SSI benefits because of disability resulting from addiction to drugs or alcohol must receive their checks through representative payees. Conditions affecting such payments are more fully discussed herein.

The SSA gives preference to social service agencies or to federal, state, or local government agencies in appointing a representative payee, unless a family member can be shown to be more appropriate.

SSI benefits are currently limited to 36 months. The period begins with the first month for which payment is made. After this period if the beneficiary continues to meet all eligibility requirements the benefits will continue for people receiving payments because of disability based on addiction to drugs or alcohol

A referral and monitoring agency (RMA) in each state issues regulations to define appropriate treatment, oversees compliance and reports to the SSA if a beneficiary is not undergoing treatment or is rehabilitated. This monitor may be a state alcohol and drug abuse agency or a state-appointed private organization.

SSI BENEFITS

SSI benefits are paid on a monthly basis. Many states cooperate with the federal government by including the state and local share of SSI payments in one check that is issued by the federal government. However, some states administer their own SSI program and issue separate checks. If a combined state and federal check is issued, the total will vary from state to state since each state sets its own benefit payment limits.

State supplemental payments are subject to frequent changes in state law. As budgets tighten, these are likely to be reduced or eliminated in the future.

It is important to apply for SSI benefits as soon as you believe you are eligible, because these benefits are paid only from the date of application or from the date of eligibility, whichever is later.

Changes in your spouse's or child's income or resources affect your benefit, and must be reported. Changes in living arrangements, such as having someone move in or out of your home, having someone in your household die, or having a baby, must be reported.

Review the income and resources lists at the beginning of the chapter; anything that changes what was on your original application should be reported, to be on the safe side. Penalties for not reporting a change or for making false statements about a change are severe. You may be subject to a fine or imprisonment or both, in addition to having to pay back any overpayment.

Any change must be reported within 10 days after the month it happens, but the change may not affect your check for the first 2 months after the event.

If you disagree with the determination made about your eligibility or the amount of your SSI payment, you have the right to appeal the decision. You also may be represented by a lawyer at any stage in your appeals. The procedure for appealing a deci-

sion is fully discussed in the section on Appeals.

The table on the next page shows the federal monthly payment amounts effective January 1999 for eligible people, both individuals and couples, in different living arrangements. The table does not include Cost-of-Living Adjustments (COLA's) or additions from state SSI programs.

Special payment rates are established for eligible people living in residential or family care facilities for the aged, the blind, the mentally disabled, or the mentally retarded. Check with your local Social Security office to find out more about these payment rates.

HOW TO APPLY FOR SSI BENEFITS

You can apply for SSI benefits at your local Social Security office. Parents, guardians, or personal representatives of eligible blind or disable children under 18, as well as personal representatives of eligible aged people who cannot manage on their own, can apply on behalf of these applicants.

The documents required to make SSI claims are listed below, although not all of these will apply to your situation. When you apply for SSI payments, you will need to take original documents with you to the Social Security office.

- Proof of age, unless that is already established because you are getting social Security benefits.
- Names of people who contribute to your support, as well as the amount of money they contribute.
- Bankbooks and statements (both checking and savings), stock certificates, and bonds.
- Latest tax return (federal and state) if you are currently employed.
- Latest tax bill or assessment notice if you own real property other than your home.
- Motor vehicle registration.
- Proof of pension and annuity payments.
- List of doctors, hospitals, or clinics where, if you are under 65, you have received treatment for blindness or disability.

Maximum Monthly Benefit Under SSI Effective January 1, 1999	
Category	**Federal Amount**
Individual living alone	$ 512
Individual living with others put paying his or her own way	512
Individual living with others and getting support and maintenance	341
Individual living in a public general hospital or Medicare-approved long-term-care facility	30
Couple living alone	769
Couple living with others but paying their own way	769
Couple living with others and getting support and maintenance	512
Couple living in a public general hospital or Medicare-approved long-term-care facility	60

• Does not include state payments or Cost-of-Living Adjustment.

Your disability review will be quicker if you encourage your health provider to send necessary medical records or if you take those records with you to the Social Security office.

Your local Social Security office offers an SSI booklet (ask for SSA publication 05-11000), or you can order it from the Government Printing Office. (410-966-7863 or 202-512-0132)

SUPPLEMENTAL SECURITY INCOME AND WELFARE

Effective August 22, 1996, the Congress of the United States enacted The Personal Responsibility and Work Opportunity Act of 1996 (Public Law 104-193) that made a number of major changes in the eligibility for and administration of the SSI program.

This Act repealed the Federal program Aid to Families with Dependent Children (AFDC) and replaced it with a new program entitled Temporary Assistance for Needy Families (TANF) which provides Block Grants to states with certified welfare plans for disbursement as time-limited cash assistance. It also made changes in child care, disability, food stamps, and supplemental security income benefits for children, legal immigrants and child support enforcement programs. Certain child nutrition programs were modified and a reduction in the Social Services Block Grants to States were included in the Act.

Under the Act, states are required to submit state welfare plans to the federal government for certification by the Department of Health and Human Services (HHS). The deadline for such submission was July 1, 1997.

More than 40 governors have submitted such plans. Thirty-seven have been certified and these states are authorized to run their own welfare and work programs with lump sums of federal money, referred to as block grants.

The states have been granted broad discretion in the establishment of different combinations of eligibility standards, penalties and benefits relating to welfare. Some states are using these grants to subsidize wages or pay housing and other expenses to help people meet their crises and avoid going on welfare.

However, states must maintain at least 75% of prior levels of state spending or lose Federal funds and those that fail to meet work requirements will have to maintain at least 80%. States that are successful in achieving the goals of the block grant in fiscal years 1998 to 2002 will be eligible for a share of a $1 billion high performance fund spread over five (5) years at the rate of $200 million per year. The act also puts a 15% administrative cap on the states' use of TANF funds for administrative activities.

The purpose of all of these changes was to encourage work by penalizing those on welfare who refuse to cooperate by cutting welfare checks, or to treat earned income in a more generous way to make sure that people are better off working than on welfare. The states have complete discretion in the methods used.

To date, half of the states that have certified plans set time limits on welfare that are stricter than the five-year lifetime limit on receiving welfare funds authorized by the federal government. Twenty-two states plan to enforce the five-year limit. Others have established two-year limits with a proviso that persons reaching the limit on payments may reapply for benefits after three (3) years off welfare. Others have set a two (2) year limit on benefits for single parents or persons caring for an incapacitated child or spouse.

At least nine states have indicated that they will treat new arrivals in the state differently than long-term residents. Such new arrivals should be aware that if they have moved from one state to another they may not qualify for benefits or receive lower benefits than in the prior state of residence and may also be required to go through a waiting period.

In Florida, the present rule permits persons to receive welfare for two years in any five-year period with a lifetime limit of five years cash assistance but if a family moves to Florida from a state with stricter limits, Florida will apply the shorter limits.

Some welfare plans will not increase payments to women who have additional children while receiving public assistance. The prior practice of increasing benefits to larger families on a routine basis has ended in many states. It is believed that such routine practice created an economic incentive for

people to have more children whom they cannot support. Pennsylvania's plan provides an exception for a family of a mother and two (2) children. Such family cannot be forced off welfare unless she earns more than $14,000 per year.

New York and Ohio plans require welfare recipients to submit to drug testing to determine whether or not they are using illicit drugs. Other states have not made up their minds on such testing. The principle behind such action is that states do not want welfare money to be used to finance the purchase of drugs and where tests are positive will require the recipient or applicant to enter into a drug rehabilitation program. Many states deny welfare benefits to people convicted of felonies involving possession, use or distribution of narcotics.

Under the new federal law, those convicted of drug crimes are generally ineligible for federal welfare benefits but states may override such ban by state law.

Most of the states that have filed state plans for certification by the federal government have indicated that they will continue to provide cash welfare benefits to "impoverished legal immigrants" who have not become citizens but who were in the United States before August 22, 1996. Those who arrived in the United States on or after August 22, 1996 are generally ineligible for Federal welfare benefits for seven (7) years.

Many of these provision in state plans will undoubtedly be modified from time to time and the above discussion of the varying terms of state plans has been presented only to inform the reader of the complexity of state requirements and the need to call the local welfare office for current eligibility requirements and limits on welfare payments in the area where the prospective applicant for benefits lives.

Telephone numbers of welfare offices in the various states are set forth in Appendix A.

SSI BENEFITS AND NONCITIZENS

Only United States citizens and nationals and certain noncitizens can receive SSI benefits.

After August 22, 1996, those who may receive SSI benefits are the following:

1. Citizens or nationals of the United States 65 years of age or older, blind or severely disabled.

2. Noncitizens 65 years of age or older, blind or severely disabled who were already receiving SSI benefits on August 22, 1996 may continue to receive them until each individual case is reviewed. The new law requires that each case be reviewed within 12 months as to eligibility under the new law. Each beneficiary will receive a letter stating what one must do to prove that they are in one of the eligible categories.

   If you can receive SSI benefits for only seven years because of your noncitizen status, the letter will state when the seven-year period ends.

   However, before the benefits are stopped you will be told how to appeal such decision and benefits will continue during the appeal.

3. Noncitizens who have been lawfully admitted to the United States for permanent residence and have a total of 40 quarters of coverage under Social Security, referred to as qualifying work credits.

   Lawful permanent residents who are credited with 40 quarters of coverage for Social Security purposes. An individual will be credited with all quarters of coverage earned by his or her parent during the period the individual was under age 18, and a married individual (including widow(er)s) with all quarters of coverage earned by his or her spouse during the marriage. However, for quarters earned after December 31, 1996, a quarter will *not* count as one of the required 40 if the non-citizen, or person whose quarters are being credited to the non-citizen, received federally funded public assistance during the quarter the work was done.

4. Certain noncitizens who are on active duty or who are honorably discharged veterans of the U.S. Armed Forces, their spouses and unmarried dependent children.

5. Certain other noncitizens may be eligible for five years after:
   - The date of admission as a refugee under Sec. 207 of the Immigration and Naturalization Service Act (INA);
   - The date granted asylum under Sec. 208 of the INA; or
   - The date deportation is withheld under Sec. 243 (h) of the INA.

6. American Indians born outside the U.S. who are under section 289 of the INA, or who are members of federally recognized Indian tribes under section 4(e) of the Indian Self-Determination and Education Assistance Act.

7. Certain noncitizens admitted as Amerasian immigrants under section 584 of the Foreign Operations, Export Financing, and Related Programs Appropriations Act, 1988. SSI eligibility is limited to the first seven years after being admitted.

8. Cuban or Haitian entrants as defined in section 501(e) of the Refugee Education Assistance Act of 1980 may be eligible for seven years from the date their status was granted.

9. Certain other noncitizens may be eligible for seven years after:
   - The date of admission as a refugee under Sec. 207 of the (INA);
   - The date granted asylum under Sec. 208 of the INA; or
   - The date deportation is withheld under Sec. 243 (h) of the INA (as in effect prior to April 1, 1997), or the date removal has been withheld under section 241(b)(3) of the INA.

Contact your local Social Security office for more detailed information about the eligibility rules for noncitizens.

If your SSI benefits stop because you are not an eligible noncitizen, you can apply again. Contact you local SSA office if you become a U.S. citizen, your immigration status changes and/or become an eligible noncitizen, or you have gained 40 qualifying work credits (because of your work and/or that of a spouse or parent). You will need to provide your naturalization certificate or other documents that show your immigration status.

Status

If you file a new application for SSI benefits, you must give proof of your U.S. citizenship or noncitizen status. Noncitizens who have served in the U.S. Armed Forces may also need to give us proof of military service. Although procedures have not been finalized, here are some examples of the kind of information you may need to provide:

■ As proof of citizenship—a U.S. birth certificate, passport, or naturalization certificate; As proof of your noncitizen status—an unexpired Form I-94 or 1551 from the Immigration and Naturalization Service (INS); or

■ As proof of military service—U.S. Military discharge papers (DD Form 214) showing honorable discharge—not based on your noncitizen status.

If you were receiving SSI as of August 22, 1996, you may also need to give proof of citizenship or noncitizen status.

If you are receiving Medicaid based on your SSI, your Medicaid should continue as long as you are eligible for SSI. If it is found that you are not eligible for SSI under the new law a letter will be sent to you about that decision.

Sponsorship

When you entered the United States, you may have had someone sign an agreement to provide support for you. This agreement is called an affidavit of support and the person who signed it is called your sponsor.

If you have a sponsor, his or her income and resources (and his/her spouse's) will generally be counted as your income and resources for a certain period of years from the time you arrive in the United States.

Your local Social Security office can give you more information about these rules and how they apply in your case.

You can get more information about becoming a citizen by writing or visiting a local Immigration and Naturalization Service

(INS) office or call 1-800-870-3676 to get an application for naturalization (N-400 Form).

Marriage To An American

New laws will affect immigrants who marry.

Immigrants are not guaranteed legal status in the United States simply by marrying—before or after the new immigration laws go into effect April 1, 1997 according to immigration lawyers and the Federal Immigration and Naturalization Service. It depends on the person and his or her immigration status. While there are exceptions in the current law and the new immigration laws, the following are the three most common situations.

■ An immigrant who enters the country legally and marries a citizen: immigration officials interview the couple several months after the wedding and, after reviewing an application, determine whether the marriage was legitimate. If so, the immigrant is granted immediate permanent residency conditional on a second interview two years later. Rather than waiting the normal five years, the immigrant may apply for citizenship after three years.

■ An immigrant who enters the country illegally and marries a citizen: the immigrant submits an application and conditional permanent residence is granted if the marriage is deemed legitimate. But they go through a second step, which amounts to applying for legal status.

This step may be expensive. After September 30, 1997 it could involve having to travel abroad to apply at an American consulate.

■ A legal or illegal immigrant who marries a permanent resident: in either case, the wait to apply for permanent residency is at least three years, but the immigrant is given a preference over others without family connections. Illegal immigrants who are waiting for legal status may be deported, if caught, whether or not they are married.

Attribution of Sponsors' Incomes and Resources

When determining SSI eligibility, the income and resources of the sponsors (and sponsors' spouses) are attributed to the noncitizen until citizenship is attained, with the following exception:

■ Attribution will end before citizenship in the case of lawful permanent residents who earn 40 quarters of coverage. Attribution for children and spouses of workers can also end before citizenship if they are credited with 40 quarters; that is, an individual would be credited with all quarters of coverage earned by his or her parent during the period the individual was under age 18, and a married individual (including a widow(er)) would be credited with all quarters of coverage earned by his or her spouse during the marriage. However, for quarters earned after December 31, 1996, a quarter will not count as one of the required 40 if the noncitizen, or person whose quarters are being credited to the noncitizen, received federally funded public assistance during the quarter the work was done.

Unlike the previous provisions, no allocation of the sponsor's income and resources is set aside for the sponsor's use, and there is no exception for individuals who become disabled after entry.

In addition to the "40 quarters" exception from sponsor-to-immigrant attribution provided for under welfare reform, provisions of the recently enacted immigration reform legislation (P.L. 102-208) exempt noncitizens whose income from all sources (including the sponsor) is not sufficient, in the absence of a cash assistance payment, to meet their need for food and shelter, and noncitizens who are bettered spouses or battered children.

Requirements For Affidavits of Support for Sponsorship

The new law requires the following in sponsoring a noncitizen:

■ In consultation with the Secretary of State and the Secretary of Health and Human Services, the Attorney General is required to develop a standard affidavit of support within 90 days after date of enactment. Effective with a date specified by the Attorney General, which will be no earlier than 60 and no later than 90 days after development of the standard affidavit, the new law requires that all newly signed affidavits be legally enforceable.

■ Affidavits of support are legally enforceable against the sponsor until the noncitizen becomes naturalized. The affidavit will be enforceable for a period of 10 years after the noncitizen last received public assistance benefits, including SSI.

■ The agency that provides assistance to a noncitizen is required to request reimbursement from the sponsor. If the sponsor does not respond or is unwilling to make reimbursement within 45 days after the agency's request, the agency may take legal action against the sponsor, and can hire individuals to collect reimbursement.

Effective upon enactment, the commissioner of the Social Security Administration (SSA) is required to furnish the name, address, and other identifying information to the INS of any individual that SSA knows is unlawfully in the United States. Such reports will be required at least four times a year. The commissioner is also required to ensure that supplementary program agreements made with states also include provisions that they also furnish such information.

For months beginning on or after the date of enactment, regardless of whether implementing regulations have been issued, the Act makes conforming changes in the medical improvement review standard to reflect the *new* definition of disability for children who file for SSI benefits.

SSA is required to issue regulations implementing the changes relating to benefits for disabled children within 3 months after the enactment date. SSA is also directed to submit to Congress all final regulations pertaining to child eligibility at least 45 days before such regulations become effective.

IMMIGRANTS AND NURSING HOMES

The Personal Responsibility and Work Opportunity Act of 1996 made many modifications in the status of immigrants and their benefits particularly under Supplemental Security Income and Medicaid programs.

In many cases, the loss of SSI benefits will affect an immigrant's right to Medicaid benefits.

Many nursing home residents have qualified for Medicaid benefits because they were receiving SSI benefits available to the needy, blind or disabled and those benefits paid for nursing home care.

Up to now Medicaid did not distinguish between the legal resident, an immigrant or a citizen.

Now nursing homes are checking the immigration status of those in the nursing home and those applying for admission to the home. They expect to exclude many elderly immigrants who become ineligible for Medicaid because of the new law.

California health officials have indicated that most illegal immigrants in nursing homes would lose their Medicaid coverage and many nursing homes are hesitant to admit anyone who is not a citizen of the United States by birth or has valid naturalization papers. This situation does not only apply to California. Other states like Texas and Florida are similarly affected because of their high levels of immigrant residents.

The federal government and the individual states share the cost of Medicaid aid with respect to immigrants. States may be faced with the problem of picking up such costs at state expense. Noncitizens in nursing homes now risk losing such benefits.

DISABILITY BASED ON DRUG ADDICTION OR ALCOHOLISM

Social Security Disability Insurance (SSDI) and Supplemental Security Income (SSI) dis-ability benefits and Medicare and Medicaid coverage based on those benefits to people who are disabled because of drug addiction and/or alcoholism are prohibited. This law applies to people who are applying for benefits or who are already getting benefits because drug addiction and/or alcoholism is a contributing factor material to their disability. Under this new law, if you are currently receiving disability benefits based on drug addiction and/or alcoholism, your cash benefits and Medicare and Medicaid based on SSI will terminate January 1, 1997. However, if you believe that you would be disabled even if you stopped using drugs and/or alcohol, you may reapply for benefits. You also will be able to appeal the decision that your disability is based on drug addiction or alcoholism.

During this time your benefits will continue to be paid to a representative payee, and you still must undergo appropriate treatment for your drug addiction and/or alcoholism, if it is available.

The following provisions apply to applications filed on or after July 1, 1996: If you receive benefits for another disabling impairment and it is found that you cannot manage your own benefits, you will be required to have a representative payee. And, if you have a drug addiction and/or alcoholism condition, you will be referred to your state drug addiction or alcoholism agency for treatment.

If benefits are sent to a representative payee, the representative payee will manage the money for you. Your representative payee may be a nonprofit social service agency or public guardian, another organization, a family member or other interested person approved by SSA to act in your best interest.

SSI ELIGIBILITY BASED ON CHILDHOOD DISABILITY

A new disability standard for new and pending applications is established for children for whom an application is made for SSI disability benefits, or whose claim is finally adjudicated, on or after the date of enactment

August 22, 1996, regardless of whether implementing regulations have been issued.

■ The "comparable severity standard" is eliminated. Instead, a child under age 18 will be considered disabled if he/she has a "medically determinable impairment," which results in marked and severe functional limitations, and which can be expected to result in death or which has lasted or can be expected to last for a continuous period of not less than 12 months.

■ The term "maladaptive behavior" in the domain of personal/behavioral function in the listing of impairments for children is eliminated and the use of an individualized functional assessment in evaluating a child's disability is discontinued.

Current Recipients

Benefits for recipients who do not meet the new childhood disability criteria terminate for the month beginning on or after July 1, 1997, or the date of the redetermination, whichever is later.

■ On or before January 1, 1997, SSA is required to notify SSI recipients whose eligibility may be affected by the new eligibility criteria.

■ Using the new criteria, SSA is required to redetermine the eligibility of these recipients no later than one (1) year after the date of enactment.

Eligibility Redeterminations and Continuing Disability Reviews (CDRs)

The following requirements apply to benefits for months beginning on or after the date of enactment, regardless of whether implementing regulations have been issued:

■ CDRs are required once every 3 years for recipients under age 18 with nonpermanent impairments; and not later than 12 months after birth for low-birth weight babies.

■ The representative payee of a child recipient whose continuing eligibility is being reviewed is required to present evidence that the recipient is receiving treatment that is considered medically necessary and available, unless SSA determines that such treatment would be inappropriate or unnecessary. If the representative payee refuses to cooperate without good cause, SSA may change the payee.

■ Eligibility redeterminations, using the adult initial eligibility criteria, must be conducted on all recipients upon attainment of age 18.

The above provisions are effective upon enactment (August 22, 1996). The Commissioner of Social Security is required to notify all potentially affected beneficiaries on the SSI rolls of this provision by March 31, 1997, and to redetermine the eligibility of all noncitizens on the SSI rolls at the time of enactment who do not meet the new eligibility date-categories previously listed, his or her eligibility will end as of the date of the redetermination decision.

Denial of SSI Benefits for 10 Years

Effective upon enactment, SSI benefits are denied for 10 years to an individual convicted in Federal or State court of having made a fraudulent statement with respect to his or her place of residence in order to receive benefits simultaneously in two or more states. Effective upon enactment:

■ SSI eligibility is denied in any month in which an individual is fleeing prosecution, is a fugitive felon, or is violating a condition of probation or parole imposed under State or Federal law.

■ SSA is required to provide, upon written request of any law enforcement officer, the current address, Social Security number (SSN), and photograph (if applicable) of any SSI recipient, provided that the request includes the name of the recipient and other identifying information, and notifies SSA that the recipient:

1. is fleeing to avoid prosecution, or custody or confinement after a felony conviction;

2. is violating a condition of probation or parole; or

3. has information that is necessary for the officer to conduct official duties, and the location or apprehension of the recipient is within the officer's official duties.

■ The new Act requires the Department of Health and Human Services (HHS) to transmit to SSA, for verification purposes, certain information about individuals and employers maintained under the Federal Parent Locator Service in an automated directory to be known as the National Directory of New Hires. SSA is required to verify the accuracy of, correct, or supply to the extent possible, and report to HHS the name, SSN, and birth date of individuals and the employer identification number of employers. SSA will be reimbursed by HHS for the cost of this verification service. State child support enforcement procedures require that the SSN of any applicant for a professional license, commercial driver's license, occupational license, or marriage license be recorded on the application. The SSN of any person subject to a divorce decree, support order, paternity determination or acknowledgment would have to be placed in the pertinent records. SSNs will also have to be recorded on death certificates.

NOTE: You can get more information 24 hours a day by calling Social Security's toll-free telephone number **1-800-772-1213**. If you want to speak to a representative, you should call between the hours of 7 A.M. and 7 P.M. on Monday through Friday. Their lines are busiest early in the week and early in the month, so it's best to call at other times. Please have your Social Security number handy when you call. Representatives can give you the address and telephone number of your local Social Security office if you would like to visit the office.

If you have a touch-tone phone, recorded information and services are available 24 hours a day, including weekends and holidays.

People who are deaf or hard of hearing may call the tollfree TTY number, 1-800-325-0778 between 7 A.M. and 7 P.M. on Monday through Friday.

The Social Security Administration treats all calls confidentially—whether they're made to the toll-free numbers or to one of its offices. They also want to be sure that you receive accurate and courteous service. That is why SSA has a second Social Security representative monitor some incoming and outgoing telephone calls.

APPEALS

The Social Security Act as amended to 1997 provides for Appeals from decisions made in connection with the receipt of benefits or the allowance of claims for reimbursement of expenses under Medicare Part A Hospital Insurance, Medicare Part B Medical Insurance, Disability and Medicare-Certified Health Maintenance Organizations (HMO's).

The Appeal Procedures for Social Security and Medicare differ in many respects. The following information may help in understanding such differences but to be certain that you are aware of any changes in the law that may occur you can obtain a free copy of "The Appeals Process" by calling 1-800-772-1213.

SOCIAL SECURITY

1. If you disagree with the computation of your Social Security benefit by the SSA a review of such determination can be obtained by requesting a Redetermination of such amount and reexamination of pertinent documents upon which the decision was made.

2. If the recomputation is not acceptable you may request a hearing by an Administrative Law Judge (ALJ) of the Office of Hearings and Appeals by filing a request in writing within 60 days from the date

the Notice of Initial Determination is received by you or your representative. The initial determination becomes final if the request is not filed within the 60-day period.

HOSPITAL (MEDICARE PART A)

1. If you disagree with the denial of coverage of a hospital bill, or continued stay in the hospital (generally denied as "not deemed medically necessary", or that sources could have been provided outside a hospital, or that such stay was for "custodial" rather than medical reasons) you can appeal such decision. These decisions are made by the Peer Review Organization (PRO) for your State.
2. The hospital will provide you with a Notice of Noncoverage and the name, address and phone number of the PRO for your state. It will also set forth the explanation of why you are being asked to leave the hospital.
3. You must have the Notice of Noncoverage to request a review by the PRO.
4. File your request for review by the PRO immediately upon receipt of the Notice of Noncoverage. Medicare will cover the expenses of your stay in the hospital while the appeal is pending. Follow the procedures described in the Notice of Noncoverage.
5. If you disagree with the PRO reconsideration decision and the amount is $200 or more, you can request a hearing by an Administrative Law Judge (ALJ). If the amount is $1,000 or more you can appeal to a Federal District Court for relief.
6. If you disagree with the Medicare-approved amount for any service you can appeal the decision by letter to the insurance carrier named in the notice, accompanied by pertinent information indicating the basis for your disagreement. The appeal must be filed within six (6) months of the date of the notice.
7. If your claim is denied and is for more than $100 you can request an Appeal hearing by the carrier (generally held at the office of your local Social Security Office). This request for hearing must be made within six (6) months of the date of receipt of the decision on the reconsideration appeal. At such time you can present evidence to support your claim. Your doctor's support of your claim is very important to your success on such appeal.
8. If the decision is resolved against you and the amount of the claim is $500 or more, you have 60 days from the date you receive the decision to request a hearing before an Administrative Law Judge (ALJ). If the amount is $1,000 or more you can appeal to an ALJ and after that decision to the Appeals Council. If you are still dissatisfied with the decision you can Appeal to the federal district court. As in prior cases, you must file a written appeal from the Appeals Council decision within 60 days after receipt of such decision. At this point, it is recommended that you obtain legal representation from a specialist in Social Security law if you have not already done so.

DISABILITY

1. The general procedures require a written request for a hearing before an ALJ with respect to a claim for benefits based on disability if a claim is denied.
2. An adjudication officer will identify the issues in dispute, develop the evidence and conduct the conference on the claim. This officer can make a decision on the claim. You can be represented by an attorney at such hearing. If no decision is made the request will be referred to an ALJ.
3. A favorable decision by the adjudication officer is binding on all parties unless either of the parties to the hearing requests that the hearing be continued, or the Appeals Council decides to review the decision on its own. The decision of the Appeals Council becomes the final decision of the SSA.

NOTE: All of these procedures are subject to change from time to time. For that reason complete, current procedures on appeals are available to the reader by writing to the Social Security Office of Hearing and Appeals, P.O. Box 3200, Arlington, VA 22203.

MEDICARE-CERTIFIED HMOs

Medicare-Certified HMOs generally operate in the same manner as ordinary HMOs providing all Medicare services to the beneficiary, except that the monthly fee is paid by Medicare to the HMO and the Medicare beneficiary has the right to multi-step appeals for the coverage of disputes, including independent review by the government.

The Federal law requires that these organizations must deliver to the enrollee a written explanation of their benefits and coverage and the right to appeal disputed claims at the time of enrollment.

The appeals process starts with the request by the patient for the HMO to reconsider its denial of services or payment for services. If the HMO refuses to reverse the decision by paying the claim or providing requested care, the HMO must send the case to the Health Care Financing Administration (HCFA) for an independent decision referred to as a "reconsideration determination." After the reconsideration determination, there are additional levels of appeal, including a hearing before an Administrative Law Judge (ALJ), an appeal to the Appeals Council of the SSA by either HMO or patient and finally a judicial review by a Federal District Court if the amount involved is $1,000 or more.

If your Medicare HMO denies a benefit to which you believe you are entitled, you should challenge that decision. The HMO must reconsider its decision within 60 days of your request and if it does not, you have a right to appeal and the HMO must send the case to the HCFA's contractor for an independent review. The HMO must provide you with specific information on how to file your appeal.

Sometimes the dispute is not about denial of services or refusal of payment for services.

It may be considered a "grievance" and you do not have the same appeal rights. The HMO in such cases is required to provide you with "Grievance Procedures" and you must follow those procedures. If you are not satisfied with the results of such procedures you can send a written complaint to your regional HCFA office for action. (Telephone numbers of regional offices of HCFA are set forth at the end of this chapter.)

You also have an alternative remedy if you are not pleased with the service of your HMO—you have the right to disenroll from the Medicare-certified HMO at any time and return to regular Medicare coverage effective on the first day of the following month. You can do so by written notice to the Medicare HMO or by completing HCFA Form 566 at your local Social Security Office. If you disenroll, you may require Medigap insurance and should time your disenrollment to coincide with the effective date of the Medigap policy.

NOTE: Before joining a Medicare-certified HMO or any other HMO you should read the HMO's materials closely, understand your rights as a Medicare beneficiary, know what benefits you are getting, what restrictions you will face and ask any questions you may have about anything that is not clear to you. Records of appeals from HMO decisions are a matter of public record and a study of such actions is available from the Public Citizens Health Research Group (202-588-1000). This record could be helpful to a prospective enrollee. One significant piece of information is that patients in for-profit HMOs were five times more likely to file an appeal to the federal government than patients in not-for-profit HMOs. Complaints concerning denials of service, payments for services, or where a patient may be liable for out-of-pocket expenses come under appeals for reconsideration. Complaints concerning delays in obtaining appointments: rudeness by doctors, and quality of care are considered "grievances" by federal authorities, are not subject to detailed, independent review process but are limited to internal HMO grievance procedures. The American Association of Health

Plans has endorsed pro-consumer measures to expedite the handling of HMO members' appeals and the HCFA has under consideration new rules that may encompass some of the following:

1. A 72-hour limit for resolving most appeals in cases where the members' lives, health or return to maximum function is at stake. Currently the complaint has been that HMOs have as long as 60 days to resolve such complaints.
2. The right to appeal decisions in areas such as prescription drug coverage, which are not part of the standard Medicare package but are offered by HMOs as an extra benefit.
3. The right to appeal decisions involving a reduction in care, such as a cutback in the frequency of speech therapy sessions, as well as terminations or outright coverage denials.

It is anticipated that such faster time limits will be available from the HCFA very soon.

CHAPTER ELEVEN
Illegal Immigrants Amnesty

In 1986, Congress enacted legislation allowing illegal immigrants who had lived "continuously" in the United States for at least four (4) years through 1986 to take steps toward legal residency.

However the Immigration & Naturalization Service (INS) stated that under the law it would deny legal status to any applicant who left the country for any length of time during the "amnesty period" without notifying INS officials.

In 1992, the Federal Court for the Ninth Circuit ruled that the INS would have to consider residency applications from illegal aliens who had not applied by the amnesty deadline in May 1988. This decision was not reversed by the Supreme Court of the United States.

However as part of the Personal Responsibility and Work Opportunity Act of 1996, Congress prohibited federal courts from hearing cases by illegal aliens who had not actually applied for the amnesty benefits by the deadline in 1988. Immigrant rights attorneys have challenged this provision as unconstitutional but such argument on appeal was rejected and the authority of the Congress to define federal court jurisdiction was recognized.

Under the new law, legal immigrants who have not become citizens are generally ineligible for food stamps and SSI benefits (see discussion under SSI) but those people who were aged, blind or disabled and were either receiving benefits or became disabled before August 22, 1996 might be permitted to receive such benefits if they were in the United States before such date. This provision would not be applicable to new immigrants.

When the Congressional action on the new budget is completed, there may be further changes on these decisions affecting immigrants if funds are available.

Currently, the state of Florida has extended Medicaid and other benefits indefinitely for legal immigrants and lawsuits have been filed by the states of Florida and New York to keep benefits for legal immigrants. Denial of such benefits, would be a tremendous burden to states like Florida, New York, California and Texas if the states were required to pick up the Federal burden of such benefits.

Some members of Congress are supporting a welfare measure that would provide funds to extend benefits to the elderly and disabled legal immigrants in certain areas of the country. It is uncertain at this time whether the final budget will provide for such relief.

Legal actions have been filed by Mayor Rudolph W. Guiliani and by lawyers for the state of Florida charging that the federal action denying such benefits to legal immigrants is unconstitutional because it forces the states to support the persons losing such benefits. It is hoped that a resolution will be found before year end.

For additional information and Naturalization Forms (N-400) call Immigration and Naturalization Office at 1-800-870-3676.

CHAPTER TWELVE
Health Maintenance Organizations: HMOs

The average American is required to make life and death decisions every day relating to the safety and health of every member of the family whether or not it is to make sure that everyone in the car has the seat belts fastened, or that the doctor or course of medical treatment chosen is the correct choice.

Everyone is living longer due to the miraculous advances in medical, surgical and pharmaceutical procedures and treatment. Diseases like tuberculosis, hepatitis, heart disease, diabetes and a myriad of other healthcare problems that in the past caused the death toll to escalate without limit can now be diagnosed early on and treated in an expeditious manner by physicians and surgeons highly trained in their professions.

When I asked people what their primary concerns were with respect to healthcare, their desire to have the best qualified doctor at the right time headed the list.

Everyone is entitled to "quality care" and the access to state-of-the-art medical and surgical technology and the right to select a doctor that they feel can really understand their healthcare problem and is competent to treat it effectively.

The elderly are living longer and like all of us require check-ups, immunizations and in some cases long-term care to make life bearable.

It is clear to everyone that as a result of progress in medical science and surgical techniques, people are living longer and the costs for hospitalization, medical treatment and surgery has escalated severely taxing existing programs like Medicare and Medicaid.

At the present time approximately 40 million persons are enrolled in Medicare, about 12% of eligible Medicare enrollees are covered by Medicare-HMOs, and 75% of those who receive health insurance through their employers are covered by some managed-care plan.

Recent coverage of high-visibility, emotionally charged healthcare problems by the press and television concerning limited hospital stays in cases of childbirth, heart surgery, mastectomies and other serious medical ailments and the lack of access to appropriate specialists has resulted in a much needed review by state legislatures and Congress to correct abuses in the delivery of healthcare and to insure that Americans are receiving "quality care." Many steps have been taken to date in these areas but they have been piecemeal rather than an overall statement of necessary criteria.

There are thousands of medical diagnoses. How long a patient should be hospitalized before it is safe to send the patient home? Is homecare necessary and available with or without medical follow-up or treatment? Should the attending physician or surgeon or the patient have the right to make such decisions?

The argument has been made that in many cases, the issue of expense and profit to the healthcare provider has taken preference over "quality care" and that the interest of investor-owned managed care plans that routinely make decisions to preserve profit may have a conflict of interest between such procedures and extended hospital care and specialized treatment of patients. Nonprofit managed care plans seem to have a better record but high-pressure competition for employer contracts and doctor-bonuses for cost-cutting are blurring the distinction between quality care and the need to curtail expenses in some cases. One survey indicated that if cutting costs or boosting profits are primary considerations then reduction of services to patients is inevitable.

For the reasons stated it is very important that the reader review carefully all of the options available to the patient under any managed care plan that is being considered to insure that the best healthcare plan for the family is being selected.

There is no question that managed care plans have become the primary choice for the delivery of health services and the trend has increased the consumers' concerns about the availability of "quality care," choice of doctors and where the power lies to decide which hospital must be used by the patient. Many state legislatures are moving faster than the federal government to regulate the industry and to calm the fears of voters.

In serving the complaints of the public, many legislatures are convinced that further steps should be taken to require plans to meet the following objectives;

1. To offer an adequate number of "available" primary doctors, specialists and hospital services within a reasonable geographic distance from the enrollee (such adequacy to be determined by each state's insurance and health departments, depending on local needs and practices).
2. To cover emergency care expenses without prior authorization if a prudent person could reasonably believe that the ailment or injury required immediate attention.
3. To provide enrollees with a clear definition of "experimental procedures" not covered by the plan.

4. To prevent plans from limiting a doctor's right to discuss with a patient optional treatments or surgical procedures or specialists for appropriate care of the patient.
5. To require plans to disclose financial arrangements between doctors and the plan to avoid possible conflict of interest with patient's rights.
6. To establish internal quality assurance programs, including ways to measure clinical procedures that would allow patients to appeal decisions by a plan to deny certain care.
7. To subject all plans to financial audits by the respective states.
8. To require plans to allow patients to see doctors outside the plan's network for an additional fee (generally referred to as "Point-of-Service" option that is rapidly becoming standard in many premium plans).
9. To require plans to provide access to all FDA approved drugs deemed necessary by the enrollee's doctor.

This legislative thinking will hopefully move healthcare forward with reasonable protection for those who use managed care plans.

In light of the foregoing, if the reader is thinking of enrolling in a managed care plan it would be appropriate to compare the proposals being considered by such legislatures with the conditions set forth in the plans being considered to see which plan contains the greater number of the benefits to meet the healthcare requirements of the family.

Many Americans want the flexibility and freedom to go to any doctor they want and they are now getting that freedom from a growing number of HMOs and managed care organizations.

Even HMOs that still require permission for various medical and surgical procedures are trying to simplify and speed up the process. A number of plans let enrollees obtain approval by telephone with approvals being given by the primary doctor or by another designated doctor or nurse. Some HMOs are anticipating legislative changes and are charging more for plans that allow visits to specialists without prior permission. In such cases, the premiums may be higher, or the patient may have to pay an extra fee if this option is used.

With managed care reaching a major percentage of the market and independent surveys of consumers showing dissatisfaction with restrictions on direct access to physicians outside the plan, prolonged waiting time for appointments when illness strikes, delays in receiving approvals to see specialists or being referred to specialists who are not taking new patients and the like, some HMOs are easing or eliminating prior approvals for some specialties such as obstetricians, cardiologists, gynecologists and others.

One of the major HMOs that pioneered plans without such restrictions or prior approvals has indicated that such plans are the fastest growing in the industry.

YOUR OPTIONS

James Firman, President of the National Council on Aging has stated that "when it comes to HMOs it is still a "buyer beware" market. The Health Care Financing Administration (HCFA) is collecting a vast amount of information and has in process an HMO cost-and-benefit comparison chart that may be available in 1998. This analysis should be very helpful to prospective enrollees in selecting a managed-care plan.

The National Committee for Quality Assurance (NCQA) evaluates and accredits various plans in managed-care and its reports may be of help. The Managed Health Care Association, representing 100 or more of the nations largest employers, and Outcomes Management System Consortium examines what enrollees are getting for the money that is spent on healthcare. Some of the reports available refer to the number of mammograms and other treatments conducted by plans but do not indicate whether the rate of correct readings of such tests was high or whether patients with positive readings were treated or survived such diagnoses. It is clear

that the current system of checks and balances should report not only what is done but also the outcome of what is done and whether what is done is effective.

One possibility for the future is to develop scorecards for most conditions and to develop a standard in medicine that can be used by individual consumers and other purchasers to compare the quality of healthcare plans. Such standards are essential to the patient but may not become effective until the state and federal governments and corporations require healthcare contracts to contain a provision.

The agenda of the Health Care Financing Administration (HCFA) contains a proposal that legislation be obtained to require "Managed Care Report Cards" detailing the strength and weaknesses in patients' care. Such "Report Cards" would, in the opinion of HCFA, lessen the criticism of "profit" vs. "quality care". It would also require verification by the plan of "current doctor lists" associated with the particular HMO or other managed care provider.

You should make sure that the doctors listed by the plan you are considering are currently available, that their patient lists do not preclude treatment of additional patients, that "gag" clauses do not restrict the delivery by doctorship information to patients of other options for treatment and that the plan does not contain limited hospital stays or other treatment for every patient, regardless of complications or other problems relating to their illness. Legislatures of many states and the federal government have already taken steps to provide such protection.

Remember, once a plan is accepted, you may find that you are under contract for a year with none of the doctors you want available for treatment.

Some plans cover specific areas and have specialists for such areas. Make sure that the specialist you may want is in your area.

Choosing between traditional health insurance plans, Medicare-eligible plans and any of the numerous managed care plans available requires a knowledge of the various types of plans and a comparison of the services they provide with the family's healthcare priorities and needs, potential expenses of any long-term illnesses and the availability of physicians, surgeons, other specialists, CAT and MRI scans, drugs or other essential services.

The patient is also a consumer and you should compare plans for extra benefits offered or additional fees charged for such services

If an HMO offers prescription coverage, ask about any benefit caps and co-payments and whether specific medications you take are on the approved HMO list.

Make a list of your uncovered medical expenses. Start with known costs of family deductibles, co-payment costs, premiums and other unreimbursable Medicare costs i.e. glasses, dental work, prescribed drugs, mental health and substance abuse services and treatment (see Medicare). Determine whether there are any other disability expenses that are not covered. Check the plan to see how many items in your list are covered. Check the plan's list of available physicians, surgeons or other specialists with whom you have a good rapport are available in your area and will accept you as a patient.

Ask the Plan Administrator about the turnover rate of doctors in the plan. A high turnover rate of 10% or more may indicate severe restrictions on doctors' recommendations for treatment or specialists. Check with the doctor of choice before enrolling in the plan to see if he or she will accept you as a patient and what the waiting time for a physical or other treatment might be.

In case of mental illness, ask whether decisions with reference to treatment are made without seeing the patient or after an examination by a specialist. Are rejections for treatment made by a doctor or by an administrator and what specialists are available and how often. Is there any limit on visits? Ask how often care is denied and on what basis.

Ask about the pre-approval procedures with respect to all specialists or other required services, how long it takes to obtain such approval whether the approval has to be in writing or oral and whether such approval is required not only from the primary physician but from the plan management as well before the cost of such services are deemed covered.

In any plan under consideration ask whether the plan has an appeals procedure relating to denial of healthcare services, length of hospital stays or the like. Some legal decisions have indicated that enrollees have specific rights: the right to written notice describing the reason for a denial of service; the right to a clear statement of how the enrollee must make an Appeal from the HMO's decision and the right of expedited consideration in time sensitive situations.

The Federal District Court of Tucson, Arizona, has ruled that the Department of Health and Human Services (HHS), which runs Medicare, is required by law to monitor HMO decisions to insure that due process for Medicare-HMO enrollees is maintained. The court also criticized some Medicare-HMOs for failing to provide enrollees with specific information about why treatments were denied. (See Appeals).

Non-Medicare HMOs tend to have more limited appeal rights than Medicare-HMOs. In any event, find out what the HMO rules are for Appeals before enrolling. Ask whether any claim or appeal you may be entitled to exercise is limited to arbitration or can a lawsuit be brought to determine your rights, and whether the plan pays your legal expenses.

HMOs: TYPES OF PLANS

Managed plans provide all of Medicare benefits and usually more with very little paperwork to be provided by the enrollee.

Usually you have to pay a fixed monthly premium and a co-payment each time a service is rendered and the premiums and co-payments, if any, will differ from plan to plan and can be changed each year. You still pay the Medicare premium but you are covered for Medicare's deductibles and co-insurance (See Medicare). There are generally no charges no matter how often you visit a doctor or are hospitalized, or have other covered services. Many plans cover preventive healthcare by providing special benefits such as eye-examinations, hearing aids, routine physicals, scheduled inoculations and prescription drugs except that there may be a minor charge for each prescription of approximately $5.00 to $20.00.

Depending on how the plan is organized, services of doctors and owner healthcare providers are delivered at a health facility or private offices of doctors who are part of the plan. The plan usually provides that you will receive care from a primary doctor (sometimes referred to as the "gatekeeper") selected by the enrollee. If a selection is not made, the plan will assign a primary doctor for you. Changes can be made by you in such selection at any time provided a doctor affiliated with the plan is selected.

All covered care must be received by the enrollee through the plan or from healthcare providers referred by the plan. If you receive services not authorized by the plan, the plan will not pay.

Medicare-Eligible HMOs

These HMOs must have a contract with Medicare in order to offer enrollment to a prospective member of the plan. Once this has been accomplished, the plan can offer two (2) types of plans:

The Risk Plan

This plan locks you into receiving all covered services through the plan or from providers referred by the plan. If services are received by you from any source not authorized by the plan, neither the plan or Medicare will pay the bill. The only exceptions recognized by such plans are for emergency services which you may receive anywhere in the United States and Canada or Mexico under special circumstances when you are temporarily outside the plan's service area, (See Medicare on services outside the U.S.) or an exception under Point Of Service (POS) options that permit you to receive certain services outside the plan's provider network of providers, in which case the plan will pay a portion of the costs of such services as set

forth in the plan. Usually you pay 20% and the plan pays 80%.

The Cost Plan

Under this plan, you are not locked in to the receipt of services through the plan or from providers referred by the plan. If you accept this plan, you can use healthcare providers associated with the plan or select providers outside the plan. If you select providers outside the plan, the plan may refuse to pay the costs of the services but Medicare will pay its share of the charges that Medicare approves (i.e., 80% of approved charges) and you will be responsible for co-insurance of 20% of such charges, deductibles and other charges in the same manner as if the enrollee had received the healthcare services under the fee for service system. If you travel a great deal from state to state, you might want to use a doctor not associated with the plan from time to time, and this plan would provide flexibility and coverage.

Enrollment In Medicare-HMO

To enroll you must be covered by Medicare Part B and pay the Part B premiums. (See Medicare.) You must reside in the plan's service area. You must not be receiving care in a Medicare-certified hospice.

Medicare-HMOs must have an advertised open enrollment period of at least 30 days once each year. Plans must enroll applicants in the order of application. You cannot be rejected because of poor health or prior illnesses.

You should select the Medicare-HMO in the area most convenient to you. If you move out of the plan's area of coverage, you will be required to reenroll or return to the Fee-For-Service Medicare or enroll in another Medicare-HMO in the enrollee's new area.

Leaving a Medicare-HMO

You can remain in a Medicare-HMO as long as it has a Medicare contract or join another plan or return to the Fee-For-Service Medicare plan. To end an enrollment, you must send a signed request to end the enrollment to the local Social Security Administration

Office. You can return to the Fee-For-Service Medicare plan the first day of the month after the Social Security office receives the request to disenroll. To move from one plan to another, you can do so at any time as long as a plan has a Medicare contract and you are automatically disenrolled from the prior plan.

NOTE: If You have a Medigap policy, you may keep the Medigap policy or when you are satisfied with the Plan, you can cancel the Medigap policy. Generally, you do not need a Medigap policy if you enter a Medicare-HMO Plan.

TRADITIONAL AND MANAGED CARE PLANS: SUMMARY

Traditional Plans

Fee-For-Service Plans

With this classic plan, patients choose their own doctors, specialists, and hospitals, and pay them directly on a fee-for-service basis. Then, the plans reimburse patients for out-of-pocket costs after the patient has paid an annual deductible and any copayment requirements. On average, traditional plans cover 80% of all medical costs above the deductible amount, and patients pay the remaining 20%. With some plans, a "stop-loss provision" kicks in if charges run very high, after which the plan covers all costs. Fee-for-service plans usually cover all care involving hospitals, including doctors and tests. Traditional plans rarely cover preventive care, such as routine physicals, well-baby care, vaccinations and birth control.

Managed-Care Plans

The Common Denominator

In these plans, healthcare is "managed" through a primary-care physician, known as a "gatekeeper" who is usually required to provide health-care services, recommend and authorize specialists and laboratory tests, and review all treatments, either short- or long-term. Financial incentives are often used to keep costs down.

Managed Indemnity

This type of plan combines traditional fee-for-service compensation with such managed-care techniques as the use of a gatekeeper to review and authorize treatment.

HMO's (Health Management Organizations)

HMOs require patients (or their employers) to pay a monthly premium to the organization to cover all medical and hospital costs. No fee for service or deductible is required, although some plans require a small copayment for service (usually five to twenty dollars). An HMO plan often focuses on preventive medicine and is less expensive than traditional health insurance plans.

There are three basic types of HMOs: In a "staff model," practitioners are employed directly by the HMO; in a "group model," a group of doctors, including primary-care physicians and specialists, is paid a given amount for each patient they agree to treat; and in a "network model," independent doctors or group practices contract with a plan to provide patient care, but often retain private, non-HMO patients as well.

The HMO pays the doctor or group a monthly fee based on the number of patients enrolled in the plan. Groups then decide how the fees will be distributed among individual doctors or their own HMO-approved doctors. The gatekeeper approves all referrals to specialists which are usually part of the HMO. Therefore, choices may be limited. HMOs also tend to discourage extensive testing, the use of specialists and extended stays in the hospital.

IPS's (Individual Practice Associations)

With this type of plan, an association called the IPA contracts with individual doctors who remain in private practice but provide care on a discounted fee-for-service basis. The scope of services covered depends on the particular plan. Because doctors stay in private practice, they see both private patients on a traditional fee-for-service as well as those covered by the IPA.

PPO's (Preferred Provider Organizations)

Doctors and other health-care providers contract with the PPO to provide care to patients at a discounted rate. Patients receive the discount as long as they see doctors associated with the PPO. They may still receive care from providers outside the plan but will receive less reimbursement from the insurance company. PPO's are offered primarily through traditional insurance companies.

EPO's (Exclusive Provider Organizations)

An EPO operates similarly to a PPO. The difference is that patients must receive all their care from the plan-affiliated doctors and specialists in order to benefit from the discounted fees. If they seek care outside the plan, they must absorb the entire cost of the treatment.

POS's (Point-of-Service Plans)

These plans permit patients to choose between insurance plans when they go for care; that is, at the point of service. As with an HMO, patients choose a primary-care doctor, or gatekeeper, from a panel of plan-affiliated doctors—the network. The gatekeeper provides direct clinical care and approves referrals to specialists. As long as patients choose providers from within the plan they pay only a token copayment or nothing. In some circumstances, if the patient goes outside the network, he will be reimbursed on a fee-for-service basis, but only in part.

OTHER MATTERS OF INTEREST ON HMOs

1. HMOs, responding to a consumer backlash and increased pressure from employers, are touting their efforts to improve the quality of care they provide through such initiatives as disease-management programs, health screenings and patient-satisfaction surveys.

    In today's health-care system, people often rely on their employer or the government to determine whether an HMO passes muster. But those enrolled or considering enrolling in an HMO can ask some questions of their own to find out whether an HMO is really trying to make people healthier.

    The government this year has begun to demand more quality information from Medicare HMOs including data on mammography, flu vaccines and follow-up care for heart attacks. Those yardsticks are part of a set of performance measures developed by the National Committee for Quality Assurance, a not-for-profit group that has come to play an increasingly important role in helping employers evaluate HMOs quality efforts.

    The committee, funded by a mix of industry, government and private sources, has granted accreditation to more than 230 HMOs and denied approval to 22 since it began reviewing plans in 1991. In evaluating quality-improvement efforts, reviewers look at health plans' ability to identify people with chronic illnesses, their programs aimed at improving clinical care and the results of patient-satisfaction surveys.

2. The most sweeping attacks on managed care have been aimed at the array of economic incentives and penalties that the industry directs at doctors, aiming to reverse what the industry says has been a tradition of excessive testing and referral to specialists.

    For example, reacting to complaints that some health maintenance organizations exclude or expel doctors for ordering tests or consultations the health plans deem unnecessary, half a dozen states—including Illinois and Georgia—have required them to include any physician who has the appropriate credentials.

    Groups in several states are taking aim at "capitation," the practice of paying physicians a set amount—the so-called capitation fee—for each health-plan member who enrolls as their patient. Under many health-organization contracts, the cost of tests or specialist treatment comes out of the primary physician's fee.

    While the earliest HMO's were essentially clinics with salaried doctors, most HMO's now are networks of physicians who follow a set of rules and typically get a monthly per-person payment. Some of the most respected HMO's pay bonuses to reward good medical results.

3. Meanwhile, 14 states have barred insurers from refusing to pay for what turn out to be "unnecessary" emergency room visits, when chest pains, for example, are traced to heartburn, not a life-threatening heart attack. And 12 states guarantee a patient's right to go directly to certain types of specialists without first getting approval from a primary care physician, who is often called a "gatekeeper."

4. At least six states have outlawed gag rules under which some health maintenance organizations threaten to dismiss doctors if they inform patients about alternative care that might add to costs. Gov. George E. Pataki of New York included a gag-rule prohibition in a recent proposal that would seek to protect patients and physicians from abuses by managed-care organizations. Similarly, in California, the State Assembly unanimously approved a gag-rule ban June 1996.

5. In an action that officials said should set a standard for the entire healthcare industry, the federal government announced rules requiring managed health plans under Medicare and Medicaid to disclose financial arrangements for physicians to the government and patients.

6. The Department of Health and Human Services said that Medicare HMO patients were entitled to all benefits available in the standard Medicare program, which pays doctors a separate fee for each service. One of those benefits, it said, was advice from doctors on "medically necessary treatment options."

So, it concluded, any contract that limits a doctor's ability to advise and counsel a Medicare beneficiary was a violation of the federal Medicare law.

Federal health officials said they intended to issue a similar policy for HMO s serving Medicaid patients.

7. *Accreditation.* A nonprofit National Committee on Quality Assurance (NCQA) evaluates HMOs according to 50 standards that measure whether a plan is set up to deliver good healthcare.

As of this date, about half the country's 630 HMOs had been reviewed.

Over 100 plans have received a full three-year accreditation; 85 earned a one-year accreditation and must make certain improvements; 26 were accredited provisionally for not meeting all NCQA standards; and 24 were denied accreditation. About 100 more plans are on the waiting list.

Also, the Joint Commission on the Accreditation of Health Care Organizations (JCAHO), which evaluates hospitals, nursing homes and other health facilities, has begun to evaluate managed-care plans (630-792-5800).

The commission was formed by the American Hospital Association and the American Medical Association.

8. *Report cards.* Some HMOs hand out report cards that rate their "performance" in certain areas of care, such as how many members had mammograms, eye exams or bypass surgery. Although the findings are based on NCQA data, critics say the data is often inconsistent, inadequate and unverified.

NCQA is working to improve these measures to collect more extensive and audited information from HMOs. Increasingly consumers will be able to learn more about patient satisfaction and plan track records in returning sick enrollees to good health.

NCQA has already compiled performance, accreditation and descriptive information on 447 HMOs in Quality Compass, a huge and growing national data base. Copies are available at many libraries, universities and companies for people who want to compare plans in their regions.

9. *Customer surveys.* How members feel about their HMOs can be a good indicator of the plan's overall quality and service. Many plans hand out consumer satisfaction surveys they conducted, but

experts say to take them with a grain of salt. It's better to look at surveys taken or audited by an independent group such as NCQA or a consumer publication.

10. For information about buying an individual plan, contact your state Health Insurance Counseling and Assistance Program (HICAP). See toll-free numbers below.

HICAPs offer free information and assistance on Medicare, Medicaid, Medigap, long-term care and other health insurance issues.

To reach HICAPs in the following states, dial 1 (800), then the number listed here:

AL	243-5463
AK	478-6065
AR	852-5494
AZ	432-4040
CA	434-0222
CO	544-9181
CT	994-9422
DE	336-9500
FL	963-5337
GA	669-8387
ID	488-5725
IL	548-9034
IN	452-4800
IA	351-4664
KS	432-3535
KY	372-2973
LA	259-5301
ME	750-5353
MD	243-3425
MA	882-2003
MI	803-7174
MN	882-6262
MO	390-3330
MS	948-3090
MT	332-2272
NV	307-4444
NH	852-3388
NJ	792-8820
NM	432-2080
NY	333-4114
NC	443-9354

ND	247-0560
OH	686-1578
OK	763-2828
OR	722-4134
PA	783-7067
RI	322-2880
SC	868-9095
SD	822-8804
TN	525-2816
TX	252-3439
UT	439-3805
VA	552-3402
WA	397-4422
WV	642-9004
WI	242-1060
WY	856-4398

For Washington D.C. call (202) 676-3900; GU (671) 475-0262; HI (808) 586-0100; NE (402) 471-2201; Puerto Rico (809) 721-8590; VT (802) 828-3302; Virgin Islands (809) 774-2991.

11. *Medicare HMOs.* The Medicare hot line and the Web site for the Health Care Financing Administration (HCFA) provide information about Medicare and managed care. Call (800) 638-6833.

Order HCFA's booklet "Medicare Managed Care" by calling (800) 638-6833

The Public Citizens Health Research Group (PCHR) completed a study of HMOs and published a rating list in its Health Letter that may be of help in answering some questions relating to HMOs. (Copies are available from PCHR, 1-800-588-1000, 1600 20th St. NW, Washington D.C. 20036. There may be a modest charge for copies.)

12. The N.Y. Office for Aging has indicated that most citizens need some assistance to cover their healthcare services and expenses under Medicare, Medicaid, Medigap or HMOs or any combination of such programs. Information is available at 212-442-1322.

13. American Medical Records Association (617-426-3660) may be of help in checking for medical records.

14. *Legal matters*. Florida cases indicate that patients will be allowed to sue HMOs in the same manner now granted to citizens to sue doctors for malpractice, for example, for failure to provide approval of appropriate treatment and specialists that results in injury or death. Suits have been instituted against doctor groups for malpractice on the basis that referral was unnecessarily delayed because its contract with the HMO gave incentives to cut back on specialized care.

   People are going to lawyers not for disputes over rare and expensive treatments, bone marrow transplants and the like but for coverage of routine care that was denied. Many cases are based on the allegation that the gatekeeper's decision limited by HMO regulations was bad medical advice.

   NOTE: Many cases have been settled through internal appeals process or through arbitration. Many HMO contracts require arbitration rather than through litigation. In any event, if the patient feels that the action by the HMO is improper, complain in writing so that it is on the record.

15. *Further information on the National Committee for Quality Assurance (NCQA).*

   As we have previously stated, NCQA has collected information from 447 of the nation's 650 health organizations, although only 292 allowed their data to be released publicly.

   The HMOs are graded in 17 areas measuring whether a consumer received the care recommended by national guidelines in 10 healthcare categories relating to breast care screenings, whether the consumers were satisfied with the particular HMO in 7 categories and speed in getting referrals to specialists.

   NCQA compares only commercial HMOs that sell policies to employers, or individuals younger than 65. However, the government is expected to release a similar report on Medicare-HMOs in early 1999. The basis for such a report will require all Medicare-HMOs to take part and supply data.

Consumers have been stymied in comparing HMOs level of care because most employers do not give the workers a choice of plans. Many consumers who choose among the health plans are concerned only with whether or not their personal doctor or hospital is in the HMO network.

At present, NCQA report is the only place consumers can go to get objective quantitative data to compare HMOs, say most health care experts.

Many large health care plans opt not to report such data.

However, many plans that publicly disclosed their data and are accredited by NCQA had better rates than those that did not.

To get better informed the reader can call NCQA at 202-955-3500 or go the the Internet www.ncqa.org for a current report.

PRESCRIPTION DRUGS AND HMOs

A sales factor that has contributed to the constant growth of HMOs of every description in the United States and elsewhere has been the offer by HMOs to cover the cost of prescription drugs—a matter of serious consideration by the elderly and others on limited budgets. However you should be aware that a plan's drug benefit program is not a guarantee that the drugs required will be on a pre-approved list or will be covered indefinitely.

Medicare-HMOs available to many elderly and retirees usually provide more generous prescription drug coverage than other plans and the government makes it easy for enrollees in such plans to switch from one Medicare-HMO to another if the selected plan fails to meet the enrollee's needs.

This ability is an important consideration because the cost of prescription drugs can seriously affect not only your health but your financial status as well.

Most HMOs offer a prescription drug benefit but many times the prescription drugs required are not covered by the plan's list of drugs approved for payment by the plan, or the cost ceiling allowed the enrollee per year may be too low to cover the drug costs of persons with chronic diseases.

The annual ceiling on drug benefits may in some plans be reduced from unlimited drug coverage to an annual cost of $1,500 or in some cases to $500 per year and in other cases to non-coverage of costs for prescription drugs not on the plan's list (sometimes referred to as "formulary"), except in rare instances when a patient's doctor requests exception for medical reasons.

It is very important that persons with congestive heart failure, diabetes, lung disease, depression, or any condition requiring constant medication be aware that the plan may not recognize particular drugs for payment, or that there may be a ceiling on costs of drugs that may in a practical sense prohibit the use of required expensive drugs. If this affects you, review your current prescription requirements and any limitations in the plan's list of approved prescription drugs with your personal physician to determine whether the current plan's list is adequate to cover your needs.

Some plans offer payment for drugs not on the plan's list but with a co-payment, or cost-sharing requirement that the patient must pay. Some plans require payment by the patient for a prescription that can be from $5.00 to $20.00 or more.

Because most prescription drugs are not covered under the Medicare program, HMOs have had great leeway to add or drop expensive drugs from their lists and to substitute medications which might require dosage reconsideration before being taken.

It is a general opinion that a switch to a "generic" version of a brand-name drug poses less potential problems than a switch from one brand-name drug to another brand-name drug that might require dosage adjustments before being taken. In such cases, check with your physician to see if any adjustment is necessary.

You might well ask what all this has to do with selecting an HMO but before enrolling in any plan you should check on the following points:

1. Ask the plan administrator for the plan's list of prescription drugs available that the plan will pay for.

2. Ask your physician about any changes in your medication that might be required if you join the plan.
3. Ask the plan administrator if its doctors or medical groups are on any kind of prescription drug budget that might put pressure on them to prescribe or approve less expensive drugs.
4. Be sure that if you need Prozac, Paxil or Zoloft, or any related drugs for depression that they are on the approved list and will be paid for. This would also be true of any drugs that you require for any chronic condition.
5. Ask whether or not the plan has a disease management program for chronic illnesses and where measures are taken to limit medication treatment for those who have chronic ailments.
6. Ask whether prescriptions can be obtained from local pharmacies, or whether they must be ordered under a mail-order program. If mail order, find out the expected time for fulfillment of the order and if the delivery of the prescription will provide required drug-interaction problem information that may disclose any problem from the drug approved.

Answers to all of the foregoing may be vital to the continued well-being and health of the enrollee in any plan.

RECENT DEVELOPMENTS ON HMOs

The Health Care Financing Administration released to the public in 1999 the following new Medicare choices available to Medicare beneficiaries.

1. Traditional Medicare (fee for service) is available for all Medicare beneficiaries.
2. Medicare provider-sponsored organizations (PSOS) run by doctors and hospitals.
3. Medicare preferred-provider organizations (PPOS) allowing members to see providers outside the network without requiring that the member must choose a primary care physician (PCP). Members can go directly to any doctor associated with the plan without prior approval of any kind.

4. Medicare private fee-for-service (PFFS) plans which are more like traditional Medicare *except* that the patient may pay more out-of-pocket expenses.

5. Medicare medical savings accounts (MSAS) which have two (2) parts: (a) An insurance policy and (b) a savings account. Medicare pays the insurance premium and deposits a net amount in the beneficiary's MSA each year to pay for health care.

NOTE: Remember that you do not have to change plans because they are available. By doing nothing, you are choosing to stay in traditional Medicare and your coverage will continue.

Suggestions

1. Choose the plan that will work for you and your family.

2. Ask questions. Will the plan you choose meet your needs for treatment, prescriptions and otherwise? Can you afford it? Are there any hidden costs?

3. If you change your mind and decide to go back to traditional Medicare will you still be able to get the same Medigap coverage?

Remember you have the right to switch to a new Medicare Option (except an MSA Plan) whenever you want until January 1, 2002.

After January 1, 2002, you will be able to choose a new Plan only "once a year" (with some exceptions) but you may not be able to get the same supplemental coverage.

You always have the right to challenge a denial of care or coverage through available appeals process.

THE INTERNET—MEDICAL INFORMATION BENEFITS AND RISKS

In the year 2000 and beyond millions of Americans will seek information on the Internet for guidance on medical treatments for a multitude of illnesses, treatments, the qualifications of doctors and specialists, available new drugs and therapies, clinical trials and experimental procedures that may be available for a variety of healthcare problems.

The reader should be aware that medical information on the Internet is not always reliable, accurate, up-to-date or appropriate in many cases.

According to a presentation by Dr. Donald Earl Henson of the National Cancer Institute relating to the Internet he stated that "although it has enormous potential to educate the public and to comfort individual patients, the Internet in some cases may actually lead to adverse medical care by spreading misleading or even fraudulent information. On the Internet there is no separation of peer-reviewed, scientifically proven conclusions from anecdotal information on personal reflections."

Another authority referring to on-line medical information, said that unregulated, unedited information on the Internet could be a recipe for disaster. It can be confusing, controversial, inaccurate, ill-advised, even deadly if the advice is followed.

The Internet can be a powerful positive partner to healthcare and a provider of patient education but doctors must help to identify or create accurate patient information web-sites to teach patients how to evaluate information about health matters found on the Internet.

The Reader should maintain an open mind, explore new information and alternative and complementary therapies but should check all information for quality and accuracy.

Check the source of the information—who put it together—the proponent's credentials—who the sponsor of the site may be—where one might obtain reliable corroborating data—check with leading medical centers, University Hospitals and Government Agencies like the National Institute of Health Centers for Disease Control and Prevention and the Food and Drug Administration.

Further check on whether the information is current and accurate—when was it released and by whom—has there been any changes since it was released—how up to date is the information.

The Web sites on health as listed on pages 125–126 that rely on peer-reviewed information and reports published in reputable medical journals that might be contracted are listed as mentioned above.

CHAPTER THIRTEEN

The Patient's Rights

THE PATIENT'S RIGHTS

All patients should be fully informed about their condition and understand the effect of any medical or surgical treatments that are recommended. Everyone has a right to such information.

There is a legal principle that is referred to as *informed consent* that healthcare professionals are obligated by law to obtain before proceeding with treatment.

Informed consent means that you agree to treatment based on your understanding of its benefits and risks. If you consent to a treatment when the doctor, hospital or healthcare service has not fully informed you of its risks and you are harmed as a result, then the doctor or service may be liable for a claim of negligence.

Printed consent forms are not legally required but are generally used in most states. Verbal consent is legally valid but if there is a disagreement between the doctor or healthcare provider with respect to the full disclosure of information with respect to a specific procedure, the written form is most likely to be accepted by a court.

The consent form must contain all the elements required for "informed consent" in addition to any relevant data that may have been discussed by the doctor or service with the patient. If you read the form and you find that something is missing or incorrect you can amend the form for accuracy.

All consent forms are not legally binding. Blanket consent forms that authorize a doctor or surgeon to perform any procedure he deems advisable are the least binding.

Many times a patient is asked to sign a consent form when checking into a hospital so that routine procedures can be carried out by hospital personnel prior to meeting with a doctor. This form does not cover medical or surgical treatment or constitute full disclosure that would support informed consent.

You should inform the doctor or service provider if a medication causes severe or allergic reaction, makes you ill, or if a device causes injury or pain. The doctor or service provider should respond to such problem to avoid possible claims for product liability or inadequate or unsafe administration of any such product or device.

THE PATIENT'S MEDICAL RECORDS

These records should contain your name, address, phone number, weight, height and other physical characteristics. They should also have an account of your medical history, family illnesses, surgeries, hospitalizations, medications that have been previously prescribed and any allergies and medications, etc. that you may have, as well as the results of physical examinations, and laboratory and x-ray results. The record would also have information on your medical condition, recommended treatment, results of such treatment and your progress, including any findings or recommendations from other doctors regarding your medical condition and treatment.

Such records would also contain any written informed consent that you may have provided relating to any recommended medical or surgical procedures or a written note explaining why you may have withheld any such informed consent.

While regulations governing such records may differ in many states, a majority of the states recognize the legal right of a patient to see and make a copy of such records. Federal laws require the government facility to provide such records under the Federal Privacy Act. Some hospitals and doctors will provide the records upon request over the phone while others may require a written request. If you are denied such request you should ask the doctor or hospital for a written statement of the reasons for such refusal. Some services may charge you for the cost of providing you with your records.

ACCESS TO INFORMATION ON DOCTORS AND SPECIALISTS

You may at some time require specific data relating to an illness or required surgery and desire a review of the background and qualifications of the physician or surgeon who has been recommended by a friend or set forth in a list provided by an HMO or other managed care service as available to you.

For those who are not computer knowledgeable, you can call MEDINET at 1-888-ASK-MEDI between the hours of 8:00 A.M. and 12:00 P.M. (Pacific Time) or call 1-800-972-6334. Or use e-mail at MEDINETINFO@askmedi.com. for information on MEDINET's products and services.

MEDINET's reports provide access to vital information about doctors in every state:

- A description of education and residency.
- American Board of Medical Specialty Certification
- States in which the physician is practicing and in which he or she is licensed to practice.
- Records of disciplinary actions taken against a physician, if any, from all states.

Terminology

It is important to note that medical board actions and terminology for minor offenses

may vary from state to state: *Letters of Concern, Public Reprimand, Consent,* or *Stipulated Agreements.*

For more serious actions there is a greater degree of uniformity. The following terms are common disciplinary actions throughout most of the United States.

- **Censure:** This is a serious sanction against the physician, and may also be accompanied by a monetary fine.

- **Probation:** This status is often accompanied by specific terms which can place serious limitations on the physician's practice. It may be for a specified duration (often measured in years) or it may be permanent. A doctor under probation is usually subject to continued monitoring by the State Board.

- **Suspension:** The physician's license has been suspended, during which time the doctor is unable to practice. Some suspensions are considered summary actions; such an emergency measure is undertaken when the situation is deemed to be an immediate threat to the public.

- **Revocation:** When a doctor's medical license to practice is revoked, this action is usually permanent. However, revocation does not always preclude a physician from practicing in other states in which they are licensed.

- **Surrender of License:** Often, to avoid confrontations with the board or prolonged legal battles, a physician will voluntarily surrender their license to practice medicine in a given state. A surrender that is considered to be with cause generally occurs while an action was pending against the physician in question.

Note that in many states, a physician whose license has been suspended or revoked by their State Medical Board may continue to practice while their case has been stayed by either the board in question, or a court of law during the appeal of said revocation or suspension.

CHAPTER FOURTEEN
Veterans Benefits

A variety of programs and benefits is available to service members and veterans of military service: disability payments, educational assistance, hospital and medical care, vocational rehabilitation, survivor and dependents benefits, special loan programs, and hiring preferences for certain jobs. Most of the veterans programs are administered by the Department of Veterans Affairs.

MONETARY BENEFITS

Two major cash benefit programs are available for veterans. The first program provides benefits to veterans with service-connected disabilities and, on the veteran's death, benefits are paid to the eligible spouse and children These benefits are not means tested—that is, they are payable regardless of other income or resources. The second program provides benefits to needy veterans who have nonservice-connected disabilities. These benefits are means tested.

Compensation For Service-Connected Disabilities

This disability compensation program pays monthly benefits to veterans whose disabilities resulted from injury or disease incurred while in or aggravated by active military duty whether in wartime or peacetime. Individuals discharged or separated from military service under dishonorable conditions are not eligible for compensation payments The amount of monthly compensation depends on the degree of disability, rated as the percentage of normal function lost. Payments range from $91 a month for a 10-percent disability to $1,870 a month for total disability. In addition, specific rates of up to $5,346 a month are paid when eligible veterans suffer certain specific severe disabilities. Veterans who have at least a 30% service-connected disability are entitled to an additional dependents allowance. The amount is based on the number of dependents and degree of disability.

Pensions For Nonservice-Connected Disabilities

Monthly benefits are provided to wartime veterans with limited income and resources who are totally and permanently disabled because of a condition not attributable to their military service. To qualify for these pensions, a veteran must have served in one or more of the following designated war periods: The Mexican Border Period, World War I, World War II, The Korean conflict, the Vietnam era, or the Persian Gulf War. The period of service must have lasted at least 90 days and the discharge or separation cannot have been dishonorable.

Effective December 1, 1996, maximum benefit amounts for nonservice-connected disabilities range from $687 per month for a veteran without a dependent spouse or child to $1,311 per month for a veteran who is in need of regular aid and attendance and who has one dependent. For each additional dependent child, the pension is raised by $117 per month. Benefits to veterans without dependents are reduced to not more than $93 per month if they are receiving long-term domiciliary or medical care from the Department of Veterans Affairs.

Benefits For Survivors

The dependency and indemnity compensation (DIC) program provides monthly benefits to the surviving spouse, children (under age 18, disabled, or students) and certain parents of service persons or veterans who die as a result of an injury or disease incurred while in or aggravated by active duty or training or from a disability otherwise compensable under laws administered by the Department of Veterans Affairs.

Dependency and indemnity compensation payments may also be made if the veteran was receiving or was entitled to receive compensation for a service-connected disability at the time of death, and if certain conditions as to the severity of the disability are met.

Eligibility for survivor benefits based on a nonservice-connected death of a veteran with a service-connected disability requires a marriage of at least a 1-year duration before the veteran's death. A surviving spouse is generally required to have lived continuously with the veteran from marriage until his or her death. Eligibility for benefits generally ends with the spouse's remarriage.

The monthly benefit amount payable to surviving spouses or veterans who died before January 1, 1993, depends on the last pay rate of the deceased service person or veteran. For pay grades E-1 through E-6, a flat monthly rate of $810 is paid to surviving spouses. Monthly benefits for grades E-7 through 0-10 range between $837 and $1,848. For veterans who died after January 1, 1993, surviving spouses receive a flat $810 a month. An additional $177 a month will be paid to supplement the basic rate if the deceased veteran had been entitled to receive 100% service-connected compensation for at least 8 years immediately preceding death. The amounts payable to eligible parents are lower and depend on: (1) The number of parents eligible, (2) their income, and (3) their marital status.

Pensions For Nonservice-Connected Death

Pensions are based on need to surviving spouses and dependent children (under age 18, disabled, or students) of deceased veterans of the wartime periods specified in the disability pension program. For a pension to be payable, the veteran generally must have met the same service requirements established for the nonservice-connected disability pension program, and the surviving spouse must meet the same marriage requirements as under the dependency and indemnity compensation program.

The pension amount depends on the composition of the surviving family and the physical condition of the surviving spouse. Pensions range from $460 a month for a surviving spouse without dependent children to $878 a month for a spouse who is in need of regular aid and attendance and who has a dependent child. The pension is raised by $117 a month for each additional dependent child.

HOSPITALIZATION AND OTHER MEDICAL CARE

The Department of Veterans Affairs provides a nationwide system of hospital and other medical care for veterans. Eligibility for any particular-medical program is based on a variety of factors. Care is furnished to eligible veterans at these facilities according to two categories: Mandatory and discretionary. Within these two categories, veterans with nonservice-connected disabilities must also have limited income and resources to be eligible for cost-free medical care from the department.

Care For Dependents and Survivors

The dependents and survivors of certain veterans may be eligible for medical care under the Civilian Health and Medical Program of the Department of Veterans Affairs (CHAMPVA) if not eligible for medical care under the Civilian Health and Medical Program of the

Uniformed Services (CHAMPUS) or Medicare. CHAMPUS is the health program administered by the Department of Defense for dependents of active duty personnel and military retirees and their dependents.

Beneficiaries covered by CHAMPVA may be treated at Department facilities when space is available. Usually, however, the person with CHAMPVA coverage is treated at a community hospital of his or her choice: The Department of Veterans Affairs pays for a part of the bill and the beneficiary is responsible for any required co-payment.

Nursing Home Care

Eligibility for admission to a Department of Veterans Affairs nursing home is the same as that for hospitalization in a Department facility. Admission is based on a priority system—with the highest priority given to veterans requiring nursing home care for a service-connected condition. The Department of Veterans Affairs also contracts with community nursing homes to provide care at Department expense to certain veterans.

Outpatient Medical Treatment

Extensive outpatient medical treatment is available to veterans: rehabilitation, consultation, training, and mental health services in connection with the treatment of physical and mental disabilities. Outpatient care is furnished according to priority groups within the resources available to the facility.

Other Medical Benefits

Other Department of Veterans Affairs programs and medical benefits are available to certain eligible veterans: domiciliary care for veterans with limited income who have permanent disabilities but who are ambulatory and able to care for themselves; alcohol and drug dependence treatment; prosthetic appliances; modifications in the veteran's home required by his or her physical condition, subject to prescribed cost limitations; and, for Vietnam-era veterans, readjustment counseling services. Under limited circumstances, the

Department may authorize hospital care or other medical services in the community at Department expense.

The Veteran Administration provides free pamphlets explaining these benefit programs. Pamphlet 27-82-2 may be ordered from the VA Compensations Group, Office of Personnel Management, Washington D.C. 20415 and FACT SHEET IS-I, Federal Benefits for Veterans and Dependents is available from the Government Printing Office Washington D.C. 20402 (202-783-3238). The VA number is 1-800-827-1000.

Women's Health:
Additional Sources of Information

I f men were asked about decision making for the family, it is the author's opinion that more than a majority would say that their wives make the main medical decisions in the family for themselves and the children. Many have stated that women seem to know that a member of the family is out of sorts, under par or sick even before that person knows it.

They read more about medical research and new developments in surgical treatments and drugs than men and having had in many cases one or more children have had more experience in hospital stays and time required for recovery than men. They feel that the more information they have the more pertinent questions can be put to the doctor about treatment and postoperative care.

In June, 1997, the *New York Times* published a survey of sources of information that while not intended as a substitute for professional consultation and advice, it was, in my opinion, an excellent presentation and deserves repeating.

Among many suggested sources the article included the following books and Internet connections that may be helpful:

THE ESSENTIAL HEART BOOK FOR WOMEN
**Dr. Morris Notelovitz and
Diana Tonnessen
(St. Martin's Griffin, 1996)**

A thorough guide to the warning signs of heart disease, the leading cause of death for women. After a primer on the heart's workings, it lays out dietary and exercise regimens for prevention.

THE COMPLETE BOOK OF BREAST CARE
**Dr. Niels H. Lauersen and Eileen Stukane
(Fawcett Columbine, 1996)**

Details the stages of breast cancer from diagnosis through treatment and recovery, and includes information on various surgeries for breast cancer, like skin-sparing mastectomy.

I'M TOO YOUNG TO GET OLD
**Dr. Judith Reichman
(Times Books/Random House, 1996)**

An overview of health concerns for women in their 40s and beyond, including fertility, menopause, urinary incontinence and hormone replacement therapy.

HARVARD WOMEN'S HEALTH WATCH
**Harvard Medical School Health
Publications Group.
Monthly (800) 829-5921**

Considered an up-to-the minute resource with articles reviewed by Harvard Medical School physicians on issues like the possible links between bone density and breast cancer and the effects of estrogen on aging skin. Regular features include nutrition updates and doctors' answers to readers' questions.

THE JOHNS HOPKINS MEDICAL LETTER,
HEALTH AFTER 50
Medletter Associates. Monthly
(800) 829-0422

Includes articles by Johns Hopkins University School of Medicine doctors on topics like pain relief for arthritis and Alzheimer's disease.

COMPLETE GUIDE TO WOMEN'S HEALTH
American Medical Association:
Dr. Ramona I. Slupik,
with Kathleen Cahill Allison
(Random House, 1996)

A straightforward guide that includes simple descriptions of body organs, medical conditions and suggested treatments.

DR. SUSAN LOVE'S BREAST BOOK
Dr. Susan Love, with Karen Lindsey
(Addison-Wesley, 1995)

This book has drawn criticism in part because Dr. Love is more skeptical than most about mammograms' usefulness and discounts some standard therapies. But many experts commend its extensive information about surgery and its non-technical style.

THE WOMEN'S COMPLETE HEALTHBOOK
American Medical Women's Association:
Drs. Roselyn Payne Epps and
Susan Cobb Stevart, eds.
(Dell Trade Paperbacks, 1995)

A broad collection of articles by female doctors that give an overview of preventive healthcare and disease diagnoses.

A NEW PRESCRIPTION FOR
WOMEN'S HEALTH
Dr. Bernadine Healy
(Penguin Books, 1995)

Drawing on her experiences from medical school to the National Institutes of Health, where she was the first female director, Dr. Healy outlines preventive measures for major threats to women's health.

BODY AND SOUL
Linda Villarosa
(Harper Perennial, 1994)

Aimed at African-American women, whose health needs differ from the general population, with chapters devoted to emotional well-being as well as topics like childbirth and AIDS.

NATIONAL WOMEN'S HEALTH REPORT
National Women's Health Resource Center
Six times a year.
Free to members of the center
(202) 293-6045

Articles explain warning signs for health conditions and advocate specific prevention methods. Also includes a physician question and answer section.

INTERNET SITES

There are thousands of sites relating to women's health on the World Wide Web. Not surprisingly, the quality of information is more varied than in books or periodicals. Here are some sites recommended by experts.

http://www.amwa-doc.org/
The site of the American Medical Women's Association includes information about women in medicine and links to pages of the American Medical Association and the Journal of the American Medical Association.

http://www.healthfinder.gov/
A web site of the Department of Health and Human Services provides direct links to online publications and data bases whose material includes consumer health information from federal agencies. This summer, the department plans to unveil a more extensive search engine, the National Women's Health Information Clearinghouse, at www.4woman.org.

http://www.mayo.ivi.com/mayo/common/
htm/womenpg.html
The Women's Health Resource Center of the Mayo Clinic's Health Oasis has articles reviewed by the clinic's doctors.

http://nhic-nt.health.org

The National Health Information Center web site. A search for the key words "women's health" turns up links to sites from a variety of reputable sources, including the American Heart Association and the National Women's Health Resource Center.

http://www.nih.gov/health

The search engine for the Women's Health Initiative of the National Institutes of Health. Searches the content of more than 100 sites within the N.I.H.

CHAPTER SIXTEEN
Food Stamps and Welfare Reform

FOOD STAMPS

The Personal Responsibility and Work Act of 1996 enacted August 22, 1996, contains provisions that change the Food Stamp program.

The program was designed to provide a means for persons with little or no income to obtain a nutritionally adequate diet. Single persons and individuals living in households meeting nationwide standards for income and assets may receive coupons redeemable for food.

The value of the coupons that a unit receives each month is determined by household size and income. Households without income receive an amount equal to 103 percent of the June monthly cost of the Thrifty Food Plan (TFP), which is a nutritionally adequate diet. This amount is updated every October for the new fiscal year to account for food price increases.

To qualify for the program, a household must have (1) less than $2,000 in disposable assets ($3,000 if one member is aged 60 or older), (2) gross income below 130 percent of the poverty guidelines for the household size, and (3) net income, after subtracting the six deductions listed below of less than 100 percent of the poverty guidelines. Households with a person aged 60 or older or a disabled person receiving either Supplemental Security Income (SSI), Social Security (OASDI), State general assistance, or veterans' disability benefits (or interim disability assistance pending approval of any of the above programs) may have gross income exceeding 130 percent of the poverty guidelines, if, after subtracting the deductions

listed below, the income is lower than 100 percent of the poverty guidelines.

The Food Stamp program is administered nationally by the Food and Consumer Service of the Department of Agriculture and operates through local welfare offices and the nation's food marketing and banking systems.

Currently, the Food Stamp program is in effect in the 50 States, the District of Columbia, Guam, and the Virgin Islands. (Since July 1982, Puerto Rico receives a block grant for nutrition assistance rather than participating in the Food Stamp program.)

These benefits are usually certified for a period of one (1) year but some states have been granted waivers allowing 2-year certification for some households. The Food Stamp program as amended by the above Act has been extended through September 30, 1997.

The Food Stamp program remains a federal program providing food to families in need of assistance. All automatic spending increases are ended, but benefits will continue to be based on the U.S. Department of Agriculture's thrifty food plan, though at 100 percent of cost rather than 103 percent as under current law. The thrifty food plan will be adjusted annually to reflect changes in the cost of food. States will be allowed to harmonize their Food Stamp program rules with those of their cash welfare block program for families receiving benefits from both programs.

Able-bodied individuals between the ages of 18 and 50 with no dependents will be required to work at least 20 hours a week or participate in a state work program in order to continue to receive food stamps for more than 3 months out of every 36-month period; an additional 3-month period of eligibility is provided for persons returning to work but later laid off.

Qualifying work programs include programs under the Job Training Act or the Trade Adjustment Assistance Act; State or local programs approved by the governor of a state, including a food stamp employment and training program; and workfare. States can encourage employers to participate in an approved wage supplementation program so that welfare recipients have an opportunity to work in real jobs.

Net income is computed by deducting the following from monthly gross income:

1. Twenty percent of earned income.
2. A standard deduction of $134 for the continental United States for fiscal year 1996 (this amount is updated October of each year)
3. The amount paid for dependent care (up to $200 a month per child under age 2 and $175 for all other dependents) while the dependent's caretaker is working or looking for work.
4. Any out-of-pocket medical expenses in excess of a $35 deductible for a person aged 60 or older or a disabled person. If more than one person in the household is aged or disabled, $35 is subtracted once before deducting combined medical expenses.
5. A child support deduction for legally-obligated child support paid for a non-household member.
6. An excess shelter deduction, which is total shelter costs including utilities minus 50 percent of income after all the above deductions have been subtracted. Effective October 1, 1995, the monthly limit is $247 for households without aged or disabled persons. Households with an aged or disabled person do not have a limit on this deduction.

Households are certified to receive food stamps for varying lengths of time, depending on their income sources and individual circumstances. Recertification is required at least annually. Households must report monthly income or expense changes of $25 or more or other changes in circumstances that would affect eligibility. Families with income or food loss resulting from disaster situations such as tornadoes or floods may be eligible for food stamps for up to 1 month if they meet the special disaster income and asset limits.

The standard deduction will remain frozen at fiscal year 1996 levels—$134 for the 48 states and the District of Columbia. The excess shelter deduction will remain capped at current-law levels through December 31, 1996—$247 for the 48 states and the District of Columbia—then rise incrementally to $300 through fiscal year 2001. Low Income Home Energy Assistance Program (LIHEAP) payments will not be counted as income. The homeless shelter allowance is maintained at current levels, and an increase in the shelter deduction over time is permitted. However, the level to which the deduction can rise is capped. The threshold above which the fair market value of vehicles is counted as an asset in determining food stamp eligibility is increased to $4,650.

To curb fraud and trafficking in the Food Stamp program, forfeiture of property is authorized, with the proceeds to be used to reimburse law enforcement officials. States are required to implement food stamp electronic benefit transfer systems by October 1, 2002, unless waived. Systems must be cost neutral over the life of the program. Within 2 years, state EBT systems shall include, to the extent practicable, retailer scanning devices that differentiate between allowable and non-allowable food items.

EARNED INCOME TAX CREDIT (EITC)

The modifications made to the EITC are intended to improve tax compliance and direct the credit to needy working families. The EITC is denied to individuals who are not authorized to be employed in the United States, or who do not have valid Social Security numbers, or have numbers assigned solely for nonwork purposes; and allows the Internal Revenue Service to use expedited procedures to correct EITC claims when there is an incorrect or missing taxpayer identification number on tax returns. The legislation also changes the definition of "adjusted gross income" used to determine the phaseout of EITC benefits, and the threshold above which an individual is not eligible as a result of having disqualified income (for example, interest, dividends, rents, royalties) has been reduced to $2,250.

MISCELLANEOUS PROVISIONS

Other provisions under welfare reform include:

■ Federal block grant funds must be expended in accordance with the laws and procedures applicable to the expenditure of the state's own resources, appropriated through the state legislature in all states, but in accordance with federal law.

■ States may test welfare recipients for use of controlled substances and may sanction those who test positive.

■ Housing benefits for fugitive felons and probation and parole violators are ended.

■ The reduction of public housing rents for persons whose income declines as a result of being sanctioned for failure to follow state welfare program requirements, such as the work requirements, is prohibited. National goals will be established to prevent out-of wedlock teenage pregnancies.

■ A mandatory appropriation of $50 million is provided annually through the Maternal and Child Health Care Block Grant to fund abstinence education programs to combat teenage pregnancy and illegitimacy.

LOW INCOME HOME ENERGY ASSISTANCE PROGRAM (LIHEAP)

The Personal Responsibility and Work Opportunity Reconciliation Act (P.L. 104-193) enacted August 22, 1996 contains provisions amending the prior law relating to LIHEAP but as amended LIHEAP is extended to 1999.

Under LIHEAP, grants are provided to the states to assist eligible households to meet the costs of home energy. In addition to the 50 states, grants were provided in fiscal year 1994 to the District of Columbia, the Commonwealth of Puerto Rico.

Energy assistance program has been administered at the federal level by HHS.

In accordance with the Act, the Secretary of HHS has left maximum policy discretion to the states. The federal information collection and reporting requirements for states were substantially reduced to require only information essential to federal administration and congressional oversight. State decisions, directed by public participation in the development of grant applications, largely replaced federal regulations.

The funds appropriated for LIHEAP provide payments to eligible households for heating or cooling costs and for home energy crises. Up to 15 percent of the available funds may be used for low-cost residential weatherization or other energy related home repairs. Grantees can request from HHS a waiver to allow up to 25 percent of available funds to be spent for low cost residential weatherization or other energy—related home repairs.

Eligibility

The unit of eligibility for energy assistance is the household, defined as any individual or group of individuals who are living together as one economic unit for which residential energy is customarily purchased in common, either directly or through rent. The Act limits payments to those households with incomes under the greater of 150 percent of the income guidelines or 60 percent of the state's median income, of those households with members receiving AFDC, SSI, food stamps, or need-tested veterans' benefits. States are permitted to set more restrictive criteria as well. Beginning with fiscal year 1986, no household may be excluded from eligibility if its income is less than 110 percent of the poverty guidelines.

Payments

States make payments directly to eligible households or to become energy suppliers on behalf of eligible households. Payments can be provided in cash, fuel, prepaid utility bills, or as vouchers, stamps, or coupons that can be used in exchange for energy supplies. Payments are to vary in such a way that the highest level of assistance is furnished to households with the lowest income and highest energy costs in relation to income, taking into account family size.

The reader should be aware that these federal provisions will be subject to modifications in the administration of benefits by the various states. For that reason it is imperative that any applicant for benefits apply to the Local State Office for applicable rules and regulations regarding the qualification for and receipt of benefits.

The location of such Medicaid Offices and applicable telephone numbers for information are listed in Appendix A.

Sources of Information

This Appendix has been compiled to provide the reader with additional sources of information relating to healthcare and general assistance.

Addresses and phone numbers for national, state and local resources are set forth to facilitate obtaining necessary documents as well as benefit information.

SOCIAL SECURITY

The Toll Free number for the Social Security Administration is 1-800-SSA-1213. You can apply for a Social Security Number, or for a Personal Earnings and Benefit Estimate Statement (PEBES) Form, or for free publications on Social Security, Retirement, Survivors' and Disability Benefits, Supplemental Security Income (SSI) and Medicare. When applying for Social Security or Medicare benefits at your local Social Security Office, you will be required to provide copies of documents establishing your age, place of birth, marriage and divorce information and certificates of death where necessary.

The following are the addresses and telephone numbers of the Office of Vital Statistics in your State from which you can obtain such documents. Each office has set up a charge for each search and the type of document. The charges listed were current when the manuscript was published but are subject to change. In many cases it is possible to charge the fees to your credit card. It is generally suggested that you obtain two copies of each document for future reference.

VITAL STATISTICS

Alabama
Center for Health Statistics
State Department of Public Health
PO Box 5625
Montgomery, AL 36103-5625
354-242-5033
$12 per copy; additional copies at same time, $4 each. Fee for special searches, $3 per hour. Birth and death records since 1908; marriage records since 1936; divorce records since 1950.

Alaska
Bureau of Vital Statistics
Department of Health and Social Services
Alaska Office Building, PO Box 110675
Juneau, AK 99811 -0675
907-465-3391
$10 per copy; additional copies at the same time, $2. Records since 1913.

Arizona
Division of Vital Records
State Department of Health
2727 West Glendale
Phoenix, AZ 85015-3887
SO2-255-3260
$9 per copy for records after 1950; earlier, $12. Records since July 1,1909; abstracts filed in counties before that date.

Arkansas
Bureau of Vital Statistics
State Department of Health
4815 West Markham
Little Rock, AR 72205
501-661-2336

$5 per copy for birth records; $4 per copy for death records. Records since February 1, 1914; some Little Rock and Fort Smith records from 1881.

California
Vital Statistics
Department of Health Services
304 S Street, PO Box 730241
Sacramento, CA 95814
916-445-2684
$13 per copy for birth record; $8 for death record. Records since July 1,1905; for earlier records, write to County Recorder in county of event.

Colorado
Health Statistics & Vital Records
State of Colorado Department of Health
4300 Cherry Creek Drive
Denver, CO 80222
303-692-2000
$15 per copy; additional copies, $6. Records since January 1, 1910; for earlier records, write to local Registrar in county of event.

Connecticut
Vital Records Unit
Department of Health Services
150 Washington Street
Hartford, CT 06106
203-566-1124
$15 per copy. Records since July 1, 1897; for earlier records, write to Town or City Hall of event.

Delaware
Office of Vital Statistics
Division of Public Health
PO Box 637
Dover, DE 19903-0637
302-739-4721
$6 for first copy; additional copies at the same time, $4 each. Records since 1881.

District of Columbia
Vital Records Branch
Room 3007
800 9th Street SW
Washington, DC 20001
202-727-5314
$12 per copy for short form; $18 for long form. Records since 1913.

Florida
Vital Statistics
Department of Health & Rehabilitative Services
PO Box 210
Jacksonville, FL 32231-0210
904-359-6900
$9 per copy; additional copies at the same time, $4 each.

Georgia
Vital Records Service
47 Trinity Avenue SW
Atlanta, GA 30334
404-656-7456
$10 per copy; additional copies, $5. Records since January 1,1919; for earlier records, write to County Health Department in county of event.

Hawaii
State of Hawaii Research & Statistics Of Office Department of Health
PO Box 3378
Honolulu, HI 96801-3378
808-586-4533
$2 per copy. Records since 1853.

Idaho
Vital Statistics
PO Box 83726
Boise, ID 83720-0036
208-334-5980
$8 per copy. Records since 1911; for earlier records, write to County Recorder in county of event.

Illinois
Division of Vital Records
605 West Jefferson
Springfield, IL 62702
217-782-6553
$10 for short form; $15 for long form; additional copies at the same time, $2 each. Records since January 1, 1916;

for earlier records, write to County Clerk in county of event.

Indiana
Division of Vital Records
State Board of Health
1330 West Michigan Street
Indianapolis, IN 46206-1964
317-383-6100
$6 per copy for birth record; $4 for death record; additional copies at the same time, $1 each. Records since October 1, 1907; death records since 1900.

Iowa
Bureau of Vital Records & Statistics
State Department of Health
Lucas State Office Building
Des Moines, IA 50319-0075
515-281-4944
$10 per copy. Records since July 1, 1880.

Kansas
Vital Statistics
Kansas State Department of Health & Environment
900 Southwest Jackson
Topeka, KS 66612
913-296-1400
$10 per copy; additional copies at the same time, $5. Birth and death records since July 1911; marriage records since 1913.

Kentucky
Office of Vital Statistics
State Department of Health
275 East Main Street
Frankfort, KY 40621
502-564-4212
$7 per copy; death records, $6. Records since January 1,1911 and earlier for Covington, Lexington, and Louisville.

Louisiana
Vital Records Section
Department of Health & Human Resources
325 Loyola Avenue
New Orleans, LA 70160
504-568-5152

$13 per copy for birth record, additional copies at the same time, $5; $7 for death record or marriage certificate. Records since 1900.

Maine
Office of Vital Records
Department of Human Services
221 State Street
Augusta, ME 04333
207-287-3181
$10 per copy; additional copies at the same time, $4 each. Records since 1892; for earlier records, write to Town Clerk in town of event.
$6 per copy. Records since 1896; for earlier records, write to City or Town Clerk in place of event.

Maryland
Division of Vital Records
State Department of Health
Mental Hygiene
PO Box 68760
Baltimore, MD 21215
410-225-5988
$4 per copy; additional copies at the same time, $3 each.

Massachusetts (except Boston)
Department of Public Health
Registry of Vital Records & Statistics
Commonwealth of Massachusetts
150 Tremont Street, Room B3
Boston, MA 02201
617-753-8600

Massachusetts (Boston)
Registry Division, Vital Statistics
Commonwealth of Massachusetts
1 City Hall Square
Boston, MA 02201
617-725-4175
$6 per copy. Records since 1639.

Michigan
State Registrar, Health Statistics
Michigan Department of Health
3423 North Logan Boulevard
PO Box 30195
Lansing, MI 48909

517-335-8656
$13 per copy; additional copies at the same time, $4 each. Search more than 3 years, $3 for each additional year. Records since 1867.

Minnesota
Registration, Department of Health
Minnesota Vital Statistics
717 Delaware Street SE
Minneapolis, MN 55414
612-623-5120
$11 per copy for birth record; $8 for death record. Records since 1900. Copies also available from Clerk of District Court in place of event.

Mississippi
Office of Vital Statistics
Department of Public Health
Mississippi State Board of Health
PO Box 1700
Jackson, MS 39215-1700
601-960-7981
$12 per copy for birth record; $7 short form; $10 for death record. Records since November 1, 1912.

Missouri (except Kansas City and St. Louis County)
Bureau of Vital Records
Missouri Department of Health
PO Box 570
Jefferson City, MO 65102-0570
314-751-6387
$10 per copy. Records since January 1910.

Missouri (Kansas City)
Bureau of Vital Statistics
City Hall
414 East 12th, 21st Floor
Kansas City, MO 64106 816-274-1428
$6 per copy.

Missouri (St. Louis County)
Bureau of Vital Statistics
St. Louis County Health Department
111 South Meramec Avenue
Clayton, MO 63105
314-854-6685
$10 per copy for birth and death records.

Montana
Division of Records & Statistics
State Department of Health & Environmental Sciences
Cogswell Building
Helena, MT 59620
406-444-2614
$10 per copy. Records since late 1907.

Nebraska
Bureau of Vital Statistics
State Department of Health
PO Box 95007
Lincoln, NE 68509
402-471-2871
$10 per copy for birth record; $7 for death record. Records since 1904; for earlier records, write to this office for information.

Nevada
Department of Health, Welfare & Rehabilitation
Division of Health, Section of Vital Statistics
505 King Street
Carson City, NV 89710
702-687-4480
$11 per copy for birth record; $8 for death record. Records since duly 1,1911; for earlier records, write to County Recorder in county of event.

New Hampshire
Bureau of Vital Records
Division of Public Health Services
Department of Health & Human Services
6 Hazen Drive
Concord, NH 03301
603-271-4650
$10 per copy, additional copies, $6. Copies of records may also be obtained from City or Town Clerk in place of event.

New Jersey
Bureau of Vital Statistics
State Department of Health
South Warren & Market Streets
Trenton, NJ 08625
609-292-4087
$4 per copy; additional copies at the same time, $2; $1 per year for search

when date is unknown. Records since June 1878; for earlier records, write to Archives and History Bureau, State Library Division, State Department of Education, Trenton, NJ 08625.

New Mexico

Vital Records Bureau
New Mexico Health & Environment Department
1190 St. Francis Drive
Santa Fe, NM 87502
505-827-2338

$10 per copy for birth record; $5 for death record. Records since 1920; for earlier records, write for information.

New York (except New York City)

Bureau of Biostatistics
Vital Records Section
State Department of Health
Empire State Plaza Corning Tower Building
Albany, NY 12237
518-474-3077

$15 per copy. Records since 1880. For records prior to 1914 in Albany, Buffalo, and Yonkers, write to Registrar of Vital Statistics in city of event.

New York (New York City, all boroughs)

Bureau of Vital Records
Department of Health
125 Worth Street
New York, NY 10013
212-788-4520/4525

$15 per copy. Records since 1866. For earlier records, write to Municipal Archives and Records Retention Center of New York Public Library, 238 William Street, New York, NY 10038.

North Carolina

Vital Records Branch
Division of Health Services
225 North McDowell Street
Raleigh, NC 27602
919-733-3526

$10 per copy, additional copies $5. Records since October 1, 1913 (and some earlier).

North Dakota

Division of Vital Records
North Dakota State Department of Health
600 East Boulevard
Bismarck, ND 58505
701-328-2360

$7 per copy for birth record; $5 for death record. Records since July 1893; records from 1894 to 1920 are incomplete.

Ohio

Division of Vital Statistics
State Department of Health
G-20 State Department Building
PO Box 15098
Columbus, OH 43215
614-446-2531

$7 per copy. Records since December 20, 1908; for earlier records, write to Probate Court in county of event.

Oklahoma

Division of Statistics
State Department of Health
PO Box 53551
Oklahoma City, OK 73152
405-271-4040

$5 per copy. Records since October 1908.

Oregon

Vital Statistics Section
Oregon State Health Division
PO Box 14050
Portland, OR 97214
503-731-4108

$15 per copy. Records since October 1903

Pennsylvania

Vital Records
512 State Office Building
300 Liberty Avenue
Pittsburgh, PA 15222
412-565-5114

$4 per copy for birth record; $3 for death record. Records since January 1, 1906; for earlier records, write to Register of Wills, Orphans' Court, county seat of event.

Rhode Island

Division of Vital Statistics

State Department of Health
101 Cannon Building
3 Capitol Hill
Providence, RI 02908
401-277-2812
$15 per copy; additional copies, $10 each. Records since 1853; for earlier records, write to Town Clerk in town of event.

South Carolina
Office of Vital Records & Public Health Statistics
Department of Health & Environmental Control
2600 Bull Street
Columbia, SC 29201
803-734-4830
$8 per copy, additional copies, $3. Records since January 1,1915; for earlier records, write to City or County Health Department in place of event.

South Dakota
Public Health Statistics
State Department of Health
445 East Capitol
Pierre, SD 57501
605-773-3355
$7 per copy. Records since July 1, 1905; some earlier records.

Tennessee
Office of Vital Records
Tennessee Department of Health & Environment
Cordell Hull Building, C-3
Nashville, TN 37247-0350
615-741-1763
$10 per copy for short form, additional copies, $2.

Texas
Bureau of Vital Statistics
Texas Department of Health
1100 West 49th Street
Austin, TX 78756
512-458-7111
$11 per copy for birth records; $9 for death records. Records since 1903.

Utah
Bureau of Vital Statistics
Utah State Department of Health
288 North 1460 West
Salt Lake City, UT 84114-2855
802-828-3286
$12 per copy for birth record; $9 for death record; additional copies at the same time, $5 each. Records since 1905; for earlier Salt Lake City or Ogden records, write to City Board of Health in city of event.

Vermont
Agency of Administration
Reference Research Section
State Administration Building
US Route 2, Drawer 33
Montpelier, VT 05633-7601
802-828-3286
$5 per copy. Records 1857–1954 (births, deaths, and marriages) and 1857-1967 (divorces). Recent records are kept by the Division of Public Health Statistics, Vermont Department of Health, PO Box 70, Burlington, VT 05402-0070; 802-862-5701.

Virginia
Division of Vital Records
State Department of Health
PO Box 1000
Richmond, VA 23208-1000
804-786-6228
$8 per copy. Records from January 1853 through December 1896 and since June 4,1912. For records between these dates, write to Health Department in city of event.

Washington
Vital Records
State Department of Health
PO Box 9709
Olympia, WA 98507
360-753-5936
$11 per copy. Records since July 1, 1907. Seattle, Spokane, and Tacoma City Health Departments also have these records; for earlier records, write to Auditor in county of event.

West Virginia
Division of Vital Statistics
State Department of Health
State Office Building No. 3
Charleston, WV 25305
304-558-2931
$5 per copy. Records since January 1917; for earlier records, write to Clerk of County Court in county of event.

Wisconsin
Center for Health Statistics
Wisconsin Division of Health
PO Box 309
Madison, WI 53701
608-266-1371
$12 per copy for birth records; $7 for death records.

Wyoming
Vital Record Services
Hathaway Building
Cheyenne, WY 82002
307-777-7591
$11 per copy for birth records; $9 for death records.

GENERAL INFORMATION SOURCES

NATIONAL ARCHIVES AND OTHER FEDERAL OFFICES

The National Archives keeps records of births, deaths, and marriages that take place at U.S. Army facilities, and of American citizens registered at foreign service posts.

Civil Archives Division
National Archives
Washington, DC 20408
202-501-5402

For registrations made less than 80 years ago on births and marriages of American citizens abroad (and for deaths after 1955), apply to Passport Services.

Atlanta
Chief Archives Branch
Federal Archives & Records Center
1557 St. Joseph Avenue
East Point, GA 30344
404-763-7477
Records cover Alabama, Florida, Georgia, Mississippi, North Carolina, South Carolina, and Tennessee. This office also hold the census records for the entire United States

Boston
National Archives—Boston Branch
Federal Records Center
380 Trapelo Road
Waltham, MA 02150
617-647-8100

Chicago
Chief Archives Branch
Federal Archives & Records Center
7358 South Pulaski Road
Chicago, IL 60629
312-581-7816

Denver
National Archives—Denver Branch
Building 20, Denver Federal Center
Denver, CO 80225
303-23-0817

Kansas City
Chief Archives Branch
Federal Archives & Records Center
2312 East Bannister Road
Kansas City, MO 64132
816-926-7271

Los Angeles
National Archives—Los Angeles Branch
2400 Avila Road
Laguna Niguel, CA 92677
714-643-4241
Records cover Arizona; the southern California counties of Imperial, Inyo, Kern, Los Angeles, Orange, Riverside, San Bernardino, San Diego, San Luis Obispo, Santa Barbara, and Ventura; and Clark County, Nevada.

New York
National Archives—New York Branch
Building 22—MOT Bayonne

Bayonne, NJ 07002-5388 201-823-7252
Records cover New Jersey, New York,
Puerto Rico, and the Virgin Islands.

Philadelphia

Chief Archives Branch
Federal Archives 7 Records Center
5000 Wissahickon Avenue
Philadelphia, PA 19144
215-597-3000
Records cover Delaware, the District of
Columbia, Maryland, Pennsylvania,
Virginia, and West Virginia.

Seattle

Chief Archives Branch
Federal Archives & Records Center
6125 Sands Point Way NE
Seattle, WA 98115
206-526-6501
Records cover Alaska, Idaho, Oregon,
and Washington.

San Francisco

Chief Archives Branch
Federal Archives & Records Center
1000 Commodore Drive
San Bruno, CA 94066
415-876-9009
Records cover California (except counties
covered by Los Angeles branch),
Hawaii, Nevada, and the Pacific
Ocean Area.

Census Records

Census records give name, age, state, territory, and country of birth for each person in a counted household. Records are available since 1790 (except for 1890, most of which were destroyed by fire).

United States Bureau of the Census
National Archives Reference Service
Washington, DC Area Office
7th and Pennsylvania Avenues NW
Washington, DC 20408
202-501-5402

Naturalization Records

The Immigration and Naturalization Service of the U.S. Department of Justice maintains records that may be useful. A search of these records requires submission of the Freedom of Information Privacy Act Request Form (G-639). To obtain a copy of the form and the location of the appropriate office(s) to submit it to, write:

U.S. Department of Justice
Immigration & Naturalization Service
Washington, DC 20536

Passport Applications

Passport applications serve as good documentation for date of birth because they show a date based on a review of the applicant's birth certificate. Passport applications from as early as 1791 through 1905 are available from the National Archives. For more recent records, write to:

Passport Services, PS/PC
Department of State
Washington, DC 20524

Military Records

Access to military records is restricted to the veteran himself or herself; next of kin if the veteran is deceased; federal officers for official purposes; or those with release authorization signed by the veteran or his or her next of kin. The form that must be submitted is Request Pertaining to Military Records, #180; it gives all the addresses of the records depositories for the different services. To obtain this form, write:

National Personnel Records Center
9700 Page Boulevard
St. Louis, MO 63132
314-263-3901

VITAL STATISTICS OFFICES

One of the duties of state and local governments is to maintain records of births, deaths, marriages, and divorce. If you no longer have original copies of the documents you need in order to file a claim with the SSA, the city, county, or state where the event was recorded can supply you with certified copies of any required documents. (It is a good idea to get at least 2 copies of anything you have to order; you will usually need them.)

See State list of Offices and telephone numbers set forth in the text for your convenience.

Social Security Regional Offices

Social Security files and records are maintained in the main office in Baltimore, Maryland, and they can usually be accessed by other offices. Regional offices serve specific areas, on a state-by-state basis. When requesting your Personal Earnings and Benefits Estimate Statement, send the form to the regional office for your state.

If your legal residence is in Alabama, Arkansas, Colorado, Illinois, Iowa, Kansas, Louisiana, Mississippi, Missouri, Nebraska, New Mexico, Oklahoma, Texas, or Wisconsin, your regional office is:

Social Security Administration
Albuquerque Data Operations Center
PO Box 4429
Albuquerque, NM 87196

If your legal residence is in Alaska, American Samoa, Arizona, California, Guam, Hawaii, Idaho, Minnesota, Montana, Nevada, North Dakota, Northern Mariana Islands, Oregon, South Dakota, Utah, Washington, or Wyoming, your regional office is:

Social Security Administration
Salinas Data Operations Center
100 East Alvin Drive
Salinas, CA 93906

If your legal residence is in Connecticut, Delaware, the District of Columbia, Florida, Georgia, Indiana, Kentucky, Maine, Maryland, Massachusetts, Michigan, New Hamp-

shire, New Jersey, New York, North Carolina, Ohio, Pennsylvania, Puerto Rico, Rhode Island, South Carolina, Tennessee, Vermont, Virginia, Virgin Islands, West Virginia, or a foreign country, your regional office is:

Social Security Administration
Wilkes-Barre Data Operations Center
PO Box 20
Wilkes-Barre, PA 18703

Fair Treatment

The SSA is committed to fair and unbiased treatment of all Social Security claimants and their representatives and has a procedure for reporting alleged bias or misconduct. You can file a complaint at any Social Security office or any of the SSA's Offices of Hearings and Appeals (OHA of offices). Your local of office can give you a copy of the complete procedures for a complaint, or write to:

Social Security Administration
Office of Hearings and Appeals
PO Box 3200
Arlington, VA 22203

REPORTING FRAUD AND ABUSES

Phony and Alarmist Mailings About Government Programs

It is illegal to send out mailings which look as though they are from the government and which may use scare tactics such as threatening the loss of Social Security or Medicare benefits. The usual aim of these mailings is to solicit money and add your name to a mailing list that can be sold. If you receive such a mailing, you should report it to:

Chief Postal Inspector
United States Post Office
475 L'Enfant Plaza SW
Washington, DC 20260-2100
202-268-2000

Medicare Fraud and Abuse

One of the reasons for the soaring cost of Medicare is the filing of fraudulent claims, estimated to account for 3% to 10% of the program's total budget. If you have reason to believe that a physician, hospital, or other healthcare provider is billing for services not performed, or is performing report it. Begin by contacting the Medicare carrier or intermediary. Then write to:

Office of the Inspector General
Department of Health and Human
  Services
OIG Hotline
PO Box 17303
Baltimore, MD 21203-7303

The OIG currently has a toll-free fraud and abuse hotline (1-800-638-5779; in Maryland, 1-800-638-3986) as do the insurance carriers, but these numbers may be abolished because of budget constraints.

This office will want to know the exact nature of the fraud you suspect; the date it occurred; the name and address of the party involved, the name and location of the carrier or intermediary you have reported it to and the date reported; and the name of the person you spoke to there and what that person told you to do.

The Consumer Information Center of the General Services Administration offers a catalog of government publications that are of special interest to consumers. The catalog includes Social Security program publications, along with many other useful and interesting booklets.

Consumer Information Center
PO Box 100
Pueblo, CO 81002
719-948-3334

If unavailable in your local office, you can order a catalog and/or any of the free "consumer" publications the SSA itself produces by writing to:

Social Security Administration
Office of Public Affairs
Public Information Distribution Center
PO Box 17743
Baltimore, MD 21235

The Government Printing Office catalog lists all of the publications currently available from the government. You can order what you want from the Printing Office, but it is sometimes easier and faster to order directly from the department that issues the publication. It's even better if you can visit a Government Printing Office bookstore—there are 24 of these around the country—where you can browse through the publications and select what is useful to you.

Government Printing Office
Order Department
Washington, DC 20402-9325
202-783-3238

MEDICARE AND OTHER MEDICAL INFORMATION

When you enroll in Medicare, you will be sent a booklet, *The Medicare Handbook,* which gives a basic description of Medicare services. (There is also a *Social Security Handbook,* but you have to buy that from the Government Printing Office, address listed above.) Here are some useful resources if you need more help with Medicare:

The Medicare Handbook contains a listing for Medicare carriers and intermediaries for your area, complete with toll-free numbers. Your doctor's office or clinic can also give you these, as can your local or state office of aging, which is listed in your phone book. This office is an excellent resource for addresses of various ombudsmen groups, such as the ones for nursing homes, the Medicare Peer Review Organizations, and the state agencies regulating home healthcare and insurance. The insurance intermediaries and PROs are also listed in the Medicare booklet.

All states, as well as the District of Columbia, Puerto Rico and the Virgin Islands, have a health insurance counseling program to give free help with Medicare, Medicaid, Medigap, long term care and other health insurance benefits. The toll-free numbers for each state are listed in *The Medicare Handbook*. These offices can help in choosing health insurance coverage, understanding your bills, claims and explanation forms.

Another resource you can write to or call is the Health Care Financing Administration at:

200 Independence Avenue SW
Washington, DC 20201
202-690-6726

The HCFA also has a toll-free number to answer questions about their programs: 1-800-638-6833. Or, you can write the Department of Health and Human Services, at the same address. The telephone number, however, is 202-690-7000.

To gain access to your own medical records, first ask the physician who treated you. If that doesn't work, the following resources may help. A free brochure (send a stamped, self-addressed envelope) entitled *Your Health Information Belongs to You* is available from:

American Medical Record Association
919 North Michigan Avenue, Suite 1400
Chicago, IL 60611

Information and advice on obtaining your medical records, including a state-by-state survey of laws governing patient access, is available for $5 from the Public Citizen Health Research Group at the address for the PCHR given above.

For a copy of your Medical Information Bureau record (if one exists), contact:

Medical Information Bureau
Information Office
PO Box 105, Essex Station
Boston, MA02112
617-426-3660

ORDERING GOVERNMENT PUBLICATIONS

In addition to the SSA's booklets and flyers, there are many other government publications that may be of interest to you. Catalogs from the following offices indicate the vast range of information available. Some, but not all, of the publications are free; the catalogs will tell you how to order.

The catalog listing the free Social Security program pamphlets found at your local SSA office is available from:

Office of Public Affairs,
SSA Distribution Center
PO Box 17743
Baltimore, MD 21235
410-965-1720

The Office of Research and Statistics for the Social Security Administration has a catalog listing and describing some of the statistical, administrative, and survey data available to non-SSA researchers.

SPECIAL RESOURCES FOR SENIORS

Recently, a nationwide information and referral service designed to identify resources available for older people at the state and local levels has been established. Administered in part by the National Association of Area Agencies on Aging, this service is called "Eldercare Locator." By dialing the toll-free number, 1-800-677-1116, callers can be referred to a local resource that will provide information about senior services available in the requested community, such as legal assistance, day care, home health services, financial aid, and nursing homes.

The network covers the United States and its territories and is a collaborative project of the Administration on Aging, the National Association of Area Agencies on Aging, and the National Association of State Units on Aging.

Anyone in the United States, Puerto Rico, and the Virgin Islands can call the toll-free number for assistance. It is a public service available business days between 9 A.M. and 8 P.M. Eastern Standard Time. It helps to have the following information when you call:

■ Your name and address, with ZIP Code, or that of the older person for whom you are calling. (The ZIP Code is key, as that is how they locate the nearest sources.)

■ A brief, general description of the problem or type of assistance you are seeking.

HCFA REGIONAL OFFICES

Additional information is available from the Regional Offices of HCFA concerning MEDICARE PART A HOSPITAL, PART B MEDICAL, SKILLED NURSING FACILITIES, HOME CARE, HOSPICES and MEDICARE-CERTIFIED HMOs.

REGION 1: BOSTON (617-565-1232) Includes CONNECTICUT, MAINE, VERMONT, MASSACHUSETTS, NEW HAMPSHIRE and RHODE ISLAND.

REGION 2: NEW YORK (212-264-8522) Includes NEW YORK, NEW JERSEY, PUERTO RICO, VIRGIN ISLANDS.

REGION 3: PHILADELPHIA (215-596-6865) Includes PENNSYLVANIA, DELAWARE, MARYLAND, VIRGINIA, WEST VIRGINIA and DISTRICT OF COLUMBIA.

REGION 4: ATLANTA (404-331-2549) Includes ALABAMA, FLORIDA, GEORGIA, KENTUCKY, MISSISSIPPI, NORTH CAROLINA, SOUTH CAROLINA, TENNESSEE.

REGION 5: CHICAGO (312-353-5737) Includes ILLINOIS, INDIANA, MICHIGAN, MINNESOTA, OHIO, WISCONSIN.

REGION 6: DALLAS (214-767-6401) Includes ARKANSAS, LOUISIANA, TEXAS, NEW MEXICO, OKLAHOMA.

REGION 7: KANSAS CITY (816-426-2866) Includes IOWA, KANSAS, MISSOURI, NEBRASKA.

REGION 8: DENVER (303-844-4024) Includes COLORADO, MONTANA, NORTH DAKOTA, SOUTH DAKOTA, UTAH, WYOMING.

REGION 9: SAN FRANCISCO (415-744-3617) Includes ARIZONA, CALIFORNIA, HAWAII, NEVADA.

REGION 10: SEATTLE (206-615-2354) Includes ALASKA, IDAHO, OREGON, WASHINGTON.

STATE MEDICAID OFFICES

More specific information on Medicaid can be obtained by requesting an "application package" for Medicaid benefits which will contain the necessary forms, a brief explanation of the Medicaid programs, and eligibility requirements. Instructions for completing the application and the assets and transfers of assets that must be shown on the application will be described therein.

ALABAMA
Dept. of Human Resources
50 Ripley Street
Montgomery, AL 36130
(205) 242-1160

ALASKA
Div. of Public Assistance
Health & Social Services Department
P.O. Box 110640
Juneau, AK 99811-0640
(907) 465-3347

ARIZONA
Dept. of Economic Security
1717 W. Jefferson
Phoenix, AZ 85007
(602) 542-4792
1-800-638-6833

ARKANSAS
Dept. of Human Services

P.O. Box 1437
Little Rock, AR 72201
(501) 682-8535

CALIFORNIA
Dept. of Social Services
(Medical)
7222 24 Street
Sacramento, CA 95822
(916) 657-3661

COLORADO
Dept. of Social Services
P.O. Box 173300
Denver, CO 80217
(303) 831-0504

CONNECTICUT
Dept. of Social Services
25 Siyourney St.
Hartford, CT 06106
(203) 424-5126

DELAWARE
Div. of Delaware State Hospital
Health & Social Services (Medicaid)
    Department
1901 N. Dupont Hwy.
New Castle, DE 19720
(302) 577-4183

FLORIDA
Economic Services
Health & Human Services
P.O. Box 13000
Tallahassee, FL 32317
(904) 488-3560

GEORGIA
Family & Children Services
Dept. of Human Resources
225 Peachtree Street, NE
Atlanta, GA 30303-2001
(404) 651-9115

HAWAII
Dept. of Human Services
100 N. Beretania St.
Honolulu, HI 98617
(808) 586-5444

IDAHO
Div. of Welfare
Dept. of Health & Welfare
450 West State Street
Boise, ID 83720
(208) 334-5747

ILLINOIS
Dept. of Public Aid
100 South Grand Ave. East
Springfield, IL 62762
(217) 782-6716

INDIANA
Dept. of Public Welfare
Government Center Building
402 W. Washington Street
Indianapolis, IN 46204
(317) 232-4705

IOWA
Bureau of Economic Assistance
Dept. of Human Services
Hoover State Office Building
Des Moines, IA 50319
(515) 281-8629

KANSAS
Income Maintenance
Dept. of Social & Rehabilitative Services
6th Fl., State Off. Bldg.
Topeka, KS 66612
(913) 296-3271

KENTUCKY
Dept. of Social Insurance
Cabinet for Human Resources
275 East Main Street
Frankfort, KY 40601
(502) 564-3703

LOUISIANA
Off. of Family Security
Health & Human Resources Department
P.O. Box 3776
Baton Rouge, LA 70821
(504) 342-0286

MAINE
Bureau of Income Maintenance
Dept. of Human Services

State House Station #11
Augusta, ME 04333
(207) 624-8200

MARYLAND
Dept. of Human Resources
Social Services Admin.
2000 Broadway
Baltimore, MD 21213
(410) 361-4600

MASSACHUSETTS
Dept. of Public Welfare
Medicaid Office
600 Washington St.
Boston, MA 02111
(617) 348-5600

MICHIGAN
Dept. of Public Welfare
235 South Cesar Chavez Ave.
Lansing, MI 48909
(517) 373-2000

MINNESOTA
Health & Human Services
444 Lafayette Road
St. Paul, MN 55155-3833
(612) 297-3933

MISSISSIPPI
Dept. of Public Welfare
P.O. Box 352
Jackson, MS 39205
(601) 359-4500

MISSOURI
Div. of Family Services
Dept. of Social Services
Box 88
615 Howerton Court
Jefferson City, MO 65103
(314) 751-4247

MONTANA
Dept. of Social
Rehabilitation Services
P.O. Box 4210
Helena, MT 59604
(406) 444-5622

NEBRASKA
Dept. of Social Services
P.O. Box 95026
Lincoln, NE 68509=5026

NEVADA
Dept. of Human Resources
Division of Welfare
505 E. King Street
Carson City, NV 89710
(702) 687-4730

NEW HAMPSHIRE
Div. of Welfare
Dept. of Health & Welfare
Hazen Drive
Concord, NH 03301
(603) 271-4321

NEW JERSEY
Div. of Public Welfare
Dept. of Human Services
6 Quakerbridge Plaza
Trenton, NJ 08625
(609) 588-2401

NEW MEXICO
Dept. of Human Services
P.O. Box 2348
Sante Fe, NM 87504
(505) 827-7256

NEW YORK
Dept. of Social Services
40 North Pearl Street
Albany, NY 12243
(518) 474-9475

NORTH CAROLINA
Dept. of Human Resources
101 Blair Drive
Raleigh, NC 27603
(919) 733-4534

NORTH DAKOTA
Dept. of Human Services
Judicial Wing
Capitol Bldg.
Bismarck, ND 58505
(701) 224-2310

OHIO
Dept. of Human Services
30 E. Broad St., 32nd Fl.
Columbus, OH 43266-0423
(614) 466-6282

OKLAHOMA
Dept. of Human Services
P.O. Box 25352
2400 Lincoln
Oklahoma City, OK 73105
(405) 521-3646

OREGON
Adult & Family Services Div.
Dept. of Human Resources
500 Summer St., N.E.
Salem, OR 97310
(503) 945-5600

PENNSYLVANIA
Dept. of Public Welfare
P.O. Box 2675
Harrisburg, PA 17105
(717) 787-2600

RHODE ISLAND
Social & Economic Services
Dept. of Social & Rehabilitative Services
600 New London Avenue
Cranston, RI 02920
(401) 464-2371

SOUTH CAROLINA
Dept. of Social Services
1535 Confederate Avenue Ext
N. Complex
Columbia, SC 29202-1520
(803) 734-5760

SOUTH DAKOTA
Office of Program Mgt.
Dept. of Social Services
700 Governor's Drive
Pierre, SD 57501
(605) 773-3165

TENNESSEE
Dept. of Human Services
1000 Second Avenue, N.
Nashville, TN 37202
(615) 532-4000

TEXAS
Dept. of Human Services
701 W. 51st St.
Austin, TX 78751
(512) 450-3030

UTAH
Office of Assistance
Payments
Dept. of Social Services
120 N. 200 W
Salt Lake City, UT 84103
(801) 538-3970

VERMONT
Dept. of Social Welfare
Agcy. of Human Services
103 South Main Street
Waterbury, VT 05671
(802) 241-2853

VIRGINIA
Dept. of Social Services
900 East Marshall
Richmond, VA 23219
(804) 780-7063

WASHINGTON
Income Assistance Services
Dept. of Social & Health Services
2100 2nd Ave.
Olympia, WA 98121
(206) 464-7060

WEST VIRGINIA
Dept. of Human Services
State Capital Complex
Bldg. 6, Rm. 617
4190 Washington St.
Charleston, WV 25313
(304) 558-4098

WISCONSIN
Div. of Community Services
Dept. of Health & Social Services
One W. Wilson Street
Madison, WI 53702
(608) 266-0554

WYOMING
Public Assistance and Social Services

Health & Social Service Dept.
Hathaway Building
2300 Capital Avenue
Cheyenne, WY 82002
(307) 777-7564

DISTRICT OF COLUMBIA
Dept. of Human Services
645 H Street, N.E.
Washington, D.C. 20002
(202) 724-5506

SOURCES OF INFORMATION: SPECIFIC DISEASES AND GENERAL ASSISTANCE

ABUSED WOMEN-NATIONAL ORG. VICTIM
  ASSISTANCE
1-800-879-6682

ACQUIRED IMMUNE DEFICIENCY
  SYNDROME (AIDS)
1-800-342-2437

AGING-NATIONAL INSTITUTE
1-800-222-4225

ALCOHOL & DRUG ABUSE CENTER
1-800-729-6686

AMERICAN HEALTH ASSOCIATION
1-800-242-8721

ARTHRITIS FOUNDATION
1-800-283-7800

ASTHMA & ALLERGIES
1-800-727-8462

BLIND, AMERICAN COUNCIL FOR
1-800-424-8666

CANCER SOCIETY
1-800-227-2345

CANCER, NATIONAL CANCER INSTITUTE
1-800-422-6237

CANCER CARE INC.
1-800-813-HOPE (4673)
website http://www.cancercareinc

CANCER RESEARCH
1-800-843-8114

CHILD ABUSE
1-800-422-4453

CROHNS DISEASE
1-800-932-2423

CYSTIC FIBROSIS
1-800-344-4823

DIABETES, NATIONAL INFO. CLEARING
  HOUSE
1-301-654-3327

DIABETES (CHILDREN)
1-800-223-1138

DIABETES, KIDNEY DISORDERS, KIDNEY
  FOUNDATION
1-800-622-9010

DOWNS SYNDROME
1-800-221-4602

ENDOMETRIOSIS
1-800-992-3636

EPILEPSY
1-800-331-1000

HEPATITIS LIVER PROBLEMS
1-800-223-0179

HOSPICE, NATIONAL ORGANIZATION
1-800-658-8898

HOSPICE
1-800-331-1620

HUNTINGTONS DISEASE
1-800-345-4372

KIDNEY TRANSPLANT, N.A. TRANSPLANT
  COORDINATING ORG.
1-913-268-9830

MENTAL HEALTH ASSOCIATION
1-800-969-6642

MISSING CHILDREN
1-800-843-5678

MULTIPLE SCLEROSIS, NATIONAL SOCIETY
1-800-344-4867

MULTIPLE SCLEROSIS
1-800-532-7667

ORGAN SHARING, UNITED NETWORK FOR
1-800-243-6667

PARKINSONS DISEASE
1-800-223-2732

RARE DISORDERS
1-800-999-6673

SICKLE CELL ANEMIA
1-800-421-8453

SPINAL CORD INJURIES
1-800-526-3456

STROKE ASSOCIATION
1-800-787-6537

SUDDEN INFANT DEATH SYNDROME
1-800-221-7437

VISITING NURSES ASSN. OF AMERICA
1-800-426-2547

INFORMATION ON ALZHEIMER'S DISEASE

The Alzheimer Association located at 919 N. Michigan Avenue, Chicago, Illinois 60611 (1-800-272-3900) having over 200 chapters and offices is an excellent source of free information relating to this problem and can refer the reader to local support groups that can answer any questions that may arise.

Other sources of information are the National Institutes of Health, 9000 Rockville Pike, Bethesda Maryland 20892 and its two divisions, National Institute on Aging (NIA) and National Institute of Neurological Disorders and Stroke (NIND&S), (1-800-352-9424) where information is available on advances in scientific understanding, plus developments that can lead to better care for the person afflicted with the disease. The Government Printing Office, Washington, D.C. 20402 (202-783-3238) can provide the reader with a detailed discussion and inventory of sources of help for Alzheimer's patients entitled "Confused Minds. Burdened Families: Finding Help for People with Alzheimer's and Other Dementias."

THE INTERNET: ADDITIONAL INFORMATION AVAILABLE ON HEALTHCARE

American Association for Cancer Research

http://www.aacr.org

This scientific society has more than 13,000 laboratory and clinical cancer researchers as members. Some areas of the site are for members only, but non-members can use the site to search for abstracts of the society's four scientific journals. Search for the words "colon cancer," for example, and the site returns dozens of abstracts. However, the articles may be difficult for lay people to understand.

CancerGuide

http://cancerguide.org/

CancerGuide: Steve Dunn's Cancer Information Page

Created by a cancer patient, CancerGuide is designed to help other cancer patients find the answers to their questions—and to figure out what questions they should be asking. The site does a good job of walking a patient through the difficult choices he or she will face. Also offers stories from other cancer patients about how they have coped. But Steve Dunn, the site's creator, does warn visitors that he is *not* a medical or health professional.

CancerNet

http://cancernet.nci.nih.gov

CancerNet has separate sections for patients, health professionals, and basic researchers. Here you can access data from PDQ, the National Cancer Institute's computer system that tracks cancer and its treatments. This is some of the most up-to-date cancer information on the Net.

CenterWatch

http://www.centerwatch.com

The Web site lists clinical trials on various diseases, including a summary of the research and information on whom to contact.

HealthFinder

http://www.healthfinder.gov

A government-sponsored site with links to more than 1,400 health sites.

HealthGate

http://www.healthgate.com/HealthGate/ MEDLINE/search.shtml

Produced by HealthGate Data Corp. of Malden, Mass., this site provides access to several medical databases, including Medline, AIDSLine and CancerLit. Enter search terms, click on the databases you want to search, and hit enter.

InteliHealth

http://www.intelihealth.com

InteliHealth, a joint venture of AETNA U.S. Healthcare Inc. and Johns Hopkins University Hospital and Health System, has content supplied by such trusted names as the National Institutes of health and the National Health Council. This site focuses on advice, ranging from what causes panic attacks to how to cure hiccups. Also includes a drug index that describes the uses and side effects of both generic and brand-name medications.

Mayo Clinic

http://www.mayohealth.org

This famous clinic's Web site provides accessible health information and allows users to E-mail questions to clinic physicians.

MedHunt

http://www.hon.ch

A medical search engine that allows users to type in key words to find appropriate sites.

Medline

http://www.ncbi.nlm.nih.gov/PubMed/

A barebones search engine, this site accesses the most useful medical information on the Web. The Medline database covers the fields of medicine, nursing, dentistry, veterinary medicine, the health-care system and preclinical studies. Unfortunately, receiving full articles is a complicated process that involves setting up a relationship with a local medical library.

Medscape

http://www.medscape.com

This Web site is used by more than 200,000 physicians, says its chairman, Peter Frishauf.

Mental Health Net

http://www.cmhc.com

Mental Health Net is a complete guide to mental-health resources on the Internet. The site indexes more than 8,000 resources, and provides sections dedicated to various disorders and illnesses. The site is published by CMHC Systems Inc., Dublin, Ohio, a company that provides software for the mental-health-care industry.

National Institutes of Health

http://www.nih.gov/health

A gateway to the extensive resources of Federal agencies, including a list of diseases being studied by the various institutes.

National Library of Medicine

http://www.nlm.nih.gov

This Web site provides access to the world's largest biomedical library, including notice of important findings issued before studies have been published. For general health information, try the library's easy-access site: http://www.nlm.nih.gov/medlineplus

RxList

http://www.rxlist.com

This online drug index, supported by a pharmacist in Benecia, Calif., allows visitors to look up a drug by either generic or brand name, find out about possible side effects, read about clinical studies and find out about any warnings. The site also includes useful information on side effects that drugs have caused in clinical trials. The site is smart enough to have "fuzzy search" capability—if you misspell the name of the drug you are seeking, it will bring up other possible matches.

The New England Journal of Medicine

http://www.nejm.org

The online version of this prestigious medical journal allows visitors to search for scientific studies the journal has published. The full text of the publication is available online only to subscribers, or to nonsubscribers by mail or fax for $10 per article. Anyone can check out the abstracts, back to 1990.

Some Basic Terms to Help Understand Managed Care

More questions are asked about what an Administrator of an HMO has said to a prospective enrollee and interpreting the language used.

CAPITATION

In Managed Care Plans a system of pre-paying doctors and hospitals a set fee to provide healthcare for each enrollee, without regard to the type or number of services rendered.

COINSURANCE

The proportion you pay for medical services under traditional insurance plans (e.g.) if a plan covers 80% of a bill, your co-insurance is 20%.

CO-PAYMENT

A fee paid by patients usually $5.00 to $10.00 for doctor visits or medical services.

DEDUCTIBLE

In some plans the amount you pay each year for medical expenses before your plan begins to pick up the expenses. Usually the lower the premium the higher the deductible.

FEE FOR SERVICE

Health coverage in which you or your insurer pays doctors and hospitals for each visit or service provided.

FORMULARY

A list of medications plans will pay for without prior approval.

GATEKEEPER

The Primary Doctor in HMO plans who may be a family practitioner, internist, obstetrician, gynecologist, pediatrician or other doctor who coordinates your basic care and recommends treatments, tests and referrals to specialists.

INDEMNITY INSURANCE

Traditional insurance that pays for specific covered services.

PRE-EXISTING CONDITIONS

Medical conditions that were present before insurance became effective. Many plans require a waiting period before they will cover pre-existing conditions.

PREMIUM

The fees you pay for your healthcare coverage.

UTILIZATION REVIEW

This is a procedure for deciding whether to approve treatment or referrals to specialists recommended by the primary doctor (GATEKEEPER). These reviews are required in many Managed Care, HMOs and Traditional Insurance Plans.

LIST OF ABBREVIATIONS

For those who may have a problem with Government abbreviations relating to programs or procedures the following will be of assistance.

AB	Aid To The Blind
ACF	Administration for Children and Families
AFDC	Aid to Families With Dependent Children
AIME	Average Indexed Monthly Wage
AMW	Average Monthly Wage
CPI	Consumer Price Index
DI	Disability Insurance
DRG	Diagnosis Related Group
ESRD	End-Stage Renal Disease
FICA	Federal Insurance Contributions Act
FY	Fiscal Year
GA	General Assistance
HCFA	Health Care Financing Administration
HHS	Department of Health & Human Services
HI	Hospital Insurance
HHA	Home Health Agency
HMO	Health Maintenance Organization
ICF	Intermediate Care Facility
JOBS	Job Opportunities and Basic Skills Training
LIHEAP	Low-Income Home Energy Assistance Program
MBC	Monthly Benefit Credited
MBR	Master Beneficiary Record
OAA	Old Age Assistance
OASDI	Old-Age, Survivors and Disability Insurance
OASI	Old-Age and Survivors Insurance
OMB	Office of Management and Budget
PIA	Primary Insurance Amount
PIB	Primary Insurance Benefit
QC	Quarter of Coverage
SECA	Self Employment Contributions Act
SMI	Supplementary Medical Insurance
SNF	Skilled Nursing Facility
SSA	Social Security Administration
SSI	Supplemental Security Income
SGA	Substantial Gainful Activity
TEFRA	Tax Equity and Fiscal Responsibility Act
VA	Department of Veterans Affairs
WIP	Work Incentive Program

Glossary

When you apply for benefits, it helps to be familiar with the terms and acronyms that are used frequently by the Social Security Administration. The Index will also help you find more information about the terms you may encounter.

Advance Directive

A document which either names in detail the measures you would (or would not) want used to prolong your life if you should be in a situation in which you could not make your wishes known, or names someone to make these decisions for you.

AIDS

Acquired Immune Deficiency Syndrome, a viral disease transmitted by bodily fluids for which there is, as yet, no known cure.

AIME

Average Indexed Monthly Earnings. The AIME is a way of defining the average monthly earnings over the life of a worker after adjusting for increases in national average earnings. A worker's AIME is the basis for determining the Primary Insurance Amount (PIA).

ALJ

Administrative law judge. The ALJ presides over hearings of Social Security appeals. Though he or she works for the Social Security Administration, the ALJ had no part in the original decision for which reconsideration of the matter is being heard.

Approved Charge

The amount determined by law to be a reasonable charge for a medical fee or service under Medicare. This set amount may be less than the provider's actual charge. You are also responsible for paying any amount above and beyond the approved charge.

ARC

AIDS-Related Complex, a group of conditions and diseases which develop as a result of a deficiency of immune cells caused by AIDS.

Auxiliary/Auxiliary Benefits

A person who, through his or her relationship to the covered worker, may be entitled to receive benefits on that worker's employment record. Benefits derived from a worker's record but paid to another (spouse, dependent child, grandchild, parent, etc.) are called auxiliary benefits.

Balance-Billing

Adopted as a part of Medicare reform, balance-billing protection holds down a patient's out-of-pocket medical costs by limiting the amount a physician can charge over and above what Medicare approves.

Basic Benefit

The base figure on which a worker's benefits are calculated. It is also called the Primary Insurance Amount (PIA) or the primary benefit.

Bend Points

Percentages of the average Indexed Monthly Earnings used as a formula for computing the Primary Insurance Amount, upon which benefits are based. Bend points are changed for each year's eligible workers according to changes in the national average earnings. Any lowering of the bend points can result in a reduction of the base upon which the benefits are computed. Also called Dollar Bend Points.

Calendar Year

Any year from January 1 through December 31, as opposed to a fiscal (accounting) year, which begins at any date in the calendar year and ends a year later.

Carriers

The private organizations—usually insurance companies—that have a contract with the government to review, then approve or deny claims and process the paperwork for Medicare Part B (medical insurance). For Medicare Part A, these companies are called intermediaries.

Catastrophic Illness

As used in the Medicare Catastrophic Protection Act passed by Congress in July 1988, this term referred to a prolonged and acute illness requiring long hospital stays and expensive treatment. The 1988 legislation provided for expanded coverage to be financed entirely by payments from Medicare beneficiaries, but this plan was so unpopular that Congress repealed the legislation in October 1989.

CDC

The Centers for Disease Control, the federal agency located in Atlanta, Georgia. The CDC issues definitions of diseases and the conditions that determine eligibility for state, federal, and/or private benefit programs.

CDR

Continuing Disability Review. People receiving disability benefits have their cases reviewed on a periodic basis to determine if disability still exists.

CMP

Competitive Medical Plan, a form of prepayment group medical practice providing health services to enrollees. See also HMO.

Coinsurance

When Medicare pays a portion of an approved charge and you (or an insurance company) pay a defined portion of that charge, the part that is not paid by Medicare is called coinsurance. The amount paid in coinsurance is counted toward your deductible. Also called cost sharing.

COLA

A Cost-of-Living Adjustment (COLA) increases benefits by a set percentage of a worker's primary benefit. Congress bases the percentage for an adjustment on increases in the Consumer Price Index (CPI). When the CPI increases between the third quarter of one year and the third quarter of the next year, barring legislative change, a COLA is automatically granted. This increase is included in the December checks received in January.

Common Law Marriage

Generally, for a common law marriage to be valid in states where they are recognized, the couple must have the intention to marry and consider themselves husband and wife. Both must be legally capable of entering into a valid marriage (of legal age and not married to someone else). A state's Attorney General's Office will furnish information about specific requirements for that state.

Coordinated Care Plan

Healthcare plans contracting with the Medicare program to provide services for

Medicare beneficiaries. But instead of paying for each service when it is delivered, Medicare prepays these groups on a monthly basis for each enrollee. This term encompasses both HMO's and CMP's.

Cost Sharing

See Coinsurance.

Covered Employment Covered Worker

Jobs in which workers (and their employers) make payroll tax contributions are considered covered employment. Over 95% of all jobs—wage or self-employed positions—are covered by Social Security and Medicare.

Credited Earnings

Credited earnings are the basis for Social Security benefits. These earnings represent no more than the maximum amount of money that is taxable each year, whether the worker is employed by an employer or is self-employed. The maximum amount of taxable earnings increases each year.

CSRS

The Civil Service Retirement System, a federal civil service retirement program. Generally speaking, federal employees hired before January 1, 1984 are covered by CSRS and those hired after that date are covered under the Federal Employees' Retirement System (FERS).

Currently Insured

You are considered currently insured if you have at least 6 credits or quarters of coverage in the 13 quarter period immediately before you die or become entitled to either disability or retirement insurance benefits. Currently insured status may ensure eligibility for certain benefits. The widow or widower of a currently insured worker may be entitled to benefits if caring for entitled children who are under 16 or disabled, or if this surviving spouse is old enough to qualify for widow's or widower's benefits.

Custodial Care

Assistance that does not require medical or paramedical training. It consists of help with activities of daily living—bathing, dressing, eating, getting in and out of bed, walking, taking medication, going to the bathroom, etc. Such care is not covered by Medicare, with the exception of hospice care.

DDS

Disability Determination Service is a state office in which a medical consultant and a disability evaluation specialist examine medical and related records to determine eligibility for disability benefits prior to the SSA ruling on eligibility. The state DDS office may request more information and/or further examinations and tests. If so, the DDS must pay any charges incurred.

Deemed Spouse

A person who entered in good faith into a marriage ceremony that was later determined to be invalid. To be eligible for benefits, the deemed spouse must be living in the same household as the covered worker at the time of application, or at the time of the worker's death (if for a survivors' benefit). In the past, such a person was not entitled to benefits if there was a legal spouse. Now, a deemed spouse is also entitled to benefits on the worker's earnings record, and the legal spouse's benefit is paid outside the maximum family benefit. That means benefits paid to a deemed spouse will not affect, or be affected by, benefits paid to others based on the worker's earnings.

Delayed Retirement Credit (DRC)

The SSA gives credit toward higher benefits to people who continue working and postpone collecting their benefits beyond the normal retirement age. For eligible people age 65 in 1996, the credit is an increase of 5% of Primary Insurance Amount for each additional year the worker delays retirement after age 65 through age 70. These percentages will increase in the future, as will the Normal Retirement Age.

Dependent

To be considered by the SSA as a dependent of a covered worker and eligible for benefits under that worker's work record, you need not be totally dependent on that worker for your support—but you must fit one of the following categories:

- Spouse, age 62 or older.
- Spouse, under age 62, caring for worker's unmarried child who is under 16 or who became disabled before age 22.
- Disabled survivor of a covered worker.
- Divorced spouse (or deemed spouse), age 62 or older, if the marriage lasted more than 10 years.
- Unmarried child under 18.
- Unmarried child, any age if severely disabled before reaching age 22, for as long as the disability continues.
- Parent or parents of a worker who can demonstrate that the worker contributes more than 50% of his, her, or their actual support.

Disability Insurance (DI)

The Social Security Disability Insurance program (DI) provides monthly cash benefits to eligible severely disabled workers. Since 1956, a portion of each year's FICA payments from contributed workers and employers has been deposit in the Disability Insurance trust.

Dollar Bend Points

See Bend Points.

DRG

Diagnostic Related Group. The government cost-containment program for Medicare which replaced the cost-plus method of payment in 1983, assigns treatment under Medicare to the appropriate Diagnostic Related Group, or DRG. Medicare pays fixed a limited fees for each of these based on local and average fees for those services.

Dual Entitlement

When a person is eligible to collect the same type of benefit under 2 different work records. About 4 of every 10 women retiring now are eligible for benefits under their own and their husband's (or former husband's) work record. Dual entitlement rules also apply to men, but only 1 percent of all male Social Security beneficiaries are eligible for a spouse's benefit that is higher than their own retirement benefit. Regardless of the number of work records under which a person is eligible, he or she can receive no more than the amount equal to the highest one.

DVA

The Department of Veterans Affairs.

Earned Income Tax Credit (EITC)

A tax credit available to some low-income workers with 1 or more dependent children (under 19 at the end of the tax year, or full-time student under 24, or permanently and totally disabled). If you qualify, use form Schedule EIC 1040 or 1040A with your tax return.

Earnings Limitation

Refers to the limit set by the SSA on how much you can earn without having your benefits reduced. Also called exempt earnings, retirement test, and earnings test threshold.

EIN

Employer's Identification Number, used by the employer when paying Social Security taxes (FICA) withheld from the employee wages.

Enrollment Periods

You must decide whether or not you want Medicare coverage and sign up for it, enroll, during specific periods. Each period has different rules.

Entitlements/Entitlement Programs

Federal programs that transfer money in the form of benefits from taxes to specific groups of people who have a legal right to these benefits because they meet certain objective criteria. Programs such as Medicaid and SSI are entitlements for which the criteria are established largely through financial need. Social Security and Medicare are also entitlements, but as the recipients of these benefits pay into the system through FICA, SECA, or Medicare premiums to help cover the costs of the programs, they are more properly thought of as social insurance.

EOMB

Explanation of Medicare Benefits, the document Medicare sends to a beneficiary when a claim is made. It explains Medicare's response to that claim.

Extended Care

Refers to services furnished in a skilled nursing facility that "extend" the care that was given during a hospital stay. Extended care is provided by, or requires the supervision of, nurses or other professionals, and is covered by Medicare only when provided in an approved skilled nursing facility.

FERS

There are three parts to the Federal Employees' Retirement System (FERS): Social Security, a federal employee pension plan, and a thrift savings plan. This retirement system covers federal employees hired after January 1, 1984 and those federal employees who joined during the period from July through December 1987.

FICA

Federal Insurance Contributions Act. The acronym FICA appears on W-2 wage forms, and shows amounts paid by wage earners into the Social Security trust funds. FICA is also referred to as the payroll tax.

Fiscal Year

The 12-month period between the settlement of financial accounts. The federal fiscal, or accounting, year begins October 1 and ends a year later on September 30. Thus FY 98 begins October 1, 1998 and ends September 30, 1999.

Fully Insured

Any worker who has earned 40 credits or quarters of coverage is considered "fully insured." A worker is also considered fully insured if he or she has earned at least 1 quarter of coverage for each year between the year of reaching age 21 and the year of death or disability, provided this is at least 6 quarters. By itself, being fully insured qualifies workers and certain family members for some, but not all, types of Social Security benefits.

HCFA

Health Care Financing Administration. It is responsible for administering the Medicare and Medicaid programs. This agency also sets the standards that hospitals, skilled nursing facilities, home health agencies, and hospices must meet to be certified as qualified providers of Medicare services. The HCFA also currently helps to regulate nursing homes.

HI

The Hospital Insurance (Medicare Part A) program. It helps pay for inpatient hospital care as well as follow-up outpatient care, some physician services, treatment of end-stage renal disease, some home care, and hospice care.

HIV

Human Immunodeficiency Virus, the virus that causes AIDS.

HMO

Health Maintenance Organization, a type of prepayment group medical practice providing health services either directly to its enrollees in a clinic or through hospitals, skilled nursing facilities, or other health suppliers. An HMO is the most closely controlled form of managed healthcare.

Hospice

Special hospitals which provide the terminally ill with physicians' services, nursing care, medical/social services, homemaker/home health services, short-term inpatient care, outpatient drugs for pain relief, and respite care. Terminally ill Medicare patients may now choose between traditional Medicare coverage or hospice care for the management of terminal illness while retaining regular Medicare coverage for all other illnesses or injuries.

Indexing

See Wage Indexing.

Insured Status

The basis on which a worker meets the qualifications for receiving benefits, which can be done in several ways. See Current Insured and Fully Insured.

Intermediaries

The organizations—usually insurance companies—that have been designated by the Health Care Financing Administration to process claims and make payments to hospitals for Medicare Part B, these organizations or companies are called carriers.

IPA

Independent Practice Associations, which have been called "HMO's without walls" have a roster of member doctors who provide care, usually on a prepaid basis.

MAGI

Modified Adjusted Gross Income, the figure used to calculate whether or not taxes are due on Social Security income. The MAGI is the total of the adjusted gross income (line 31 of IRS 1040) plus tax-exempt income and one-half the total

of the year's Social Security benefits received by an individual, or couple.

Managed Healthcare

A catchall phrase for plans which exert control over costs of healthcare delivery, either by contracting with suppliers to furnish care to groups on a prepaid basis (HMO's) or through traditional insured or employer-paid plans which require review for hospital admission, surgery, etc.

Maximum Allowable Amount

Depending on your age, the maximum amount you are allowed to earn without lowering or eliminating your benefit.

Maximum Family Benefit

The maximum monthly amount that can be paid to one family on a worker's earning record, usually between 150% and 180% of the worker's PIA. Your maximum family benefit is shown on your Personal Earnings and Benefit Estimate Statement.

Means Test

Method of determining whether the income and/or assets of an applicant for government public assistance (welfare) benefit are low enough to qualify for needs-based programs such as SSI and Medicaid.

Medigap Insurance

The catchall term for insurance policies which cover healthcare services not covered by Medicare. Abuse in this area has become so widespread, Congress passed a law governing what can be offered and to whom it can be sold.

Minimum Benefit

A special benefit payable to people in covered employment for many years at very low earnings. This benefit is computed by using an alternative benefit formula for such workers. This minimum is paid if it is greater than the benefit computed under another method. COLA's are added to the minimum benefit.

Modified Adjusted Gross Income

See MAGI.

Monthly Earnings Test

In the first year in which you retire, you can receive the full amount of your benefits for any month in which you don't earn the maximum allowable amount, or the exempt earnings, for your age group. If you are self-employed, you may get your full benefit for any month in which you do not perform substantial services—usually, that means work in your business for less than 45 hours during the month. (After the first year, earnings as well as benefits are calculated on a yearly basis.)

Normal Retirement Age (NRA)

Age at which the SSA will begin to pay full (unreduced) retirement benefits. Presently, the NRA is 65, but it will begin to rise (affecting those who become 62 in 2000) gradually until it reaches age 67 in 2027.

Notch

Some workers born in or before 1916 whose benefits were figured under the method in effect before 1977 receive slightly higher benefits than the workers born between 1917 and 1921 (the so-called "notch babies") who have similar earnings histories and who retired at the same age. Some definitions extend the notch to 1926. This unintended small windfall for the older workers came about through the introduction of COLA's in 1972.

OHA

The Social Security Administration's Office of Hearings and Appeals.

OMB

The Office of Management and Budget.

Ombudsman

Government-appointed officials whose purpose is to look after the interests and protect the rights of specific groups of people. An example is the Medicare Peer Review Organizations. Some private groups, such as the American Association of Retired Persons (AARP), have special committees that perform similar functions.

PASS

Plan for Achieving Self-Support, a program to encourage people receiving SSI and disability payments to rejoin the workforce through individualized plans for training and support in job placement.

PEBES

Personal Earnings and Benefit Estimate Statement. By using computerized records of your past covered earnings and your own information about your expected future earnings, the SSA can give you an estimate of your Social Security benefit at the time you choose to receive it. Your local SSA office has forms on which to request the estimate, or call 1-800-772-1213.

Permitted Disparity

Also called Social Security integration under federal pension and tax laws, companies paying pensions are specifically allowed to include the amount of a worker's Social Security benefit when calculating total retirement benefit. Currently, the law limits the reduction of a pension to no more than 50% for pension credits earned after December 31, 1988; it can be as much as 100% of credits earned before that date.

PIA

Primary Insurance Amount, also called primary benefit and basic benefit. All (100%) of this amount paid to an entitled worker when he or she retires at the Normal Retirement Age—or this is the amount that is reduced by a sliding percentage for earlier retirement. This is also the amount on which benefits payable to a worker's dependents and survivors are calculated.

Poverty Level Poverty Threshold

Each year, the SSA sets figures for income below which the recipients are officially considered to be living in poverty. The income figures are set for incomes of an aged individual, a family of 2 with an aged head, and families of different sizes.

PPO

Preferred Provider Organization. A more loosely organized managed healthcare network, which provides a list of doctors and hospitals. It pays more if you go to a preferred provider, less if you don't.

Preventive Medicine

Treatment by healthcare providers which attempts to prevent infirmity and disease rather than treating illness after it has occurred.

Primary Wage Earner

One whose earnings record is used to determine benefits payable to himself or herself or to eligible dependents and survivors. A primary wage earner can be an employee a self-employed worker.

PRO

Peer Review Organizations are groups of physicians paid by the federal government to review medical care given to Medicare patients by hospitals and other physicians. PRO's in each state provide a professional group to oversee the cost-cutting goals authorized by Medicare, to maintain standards and to guard against abuses.

Provider

The hospital, nursing facility, or healthcare professional providing Medicare service equipment.

Provisional Income

An individual's or married couple's adjusted gross income as reported on the IRS Form 1040, plus 50% of total Social Security benefits received for the year, plus nontaxable interest. If this sum exceeds base amounts (set yearly), federal income tax must be paid on Social Security benefits.

QC

Quarter of Coverage, a unit of work credit used by the SSA to calculate benefits. The number of credits you need depends on the kind of benefit you are claiming, as well as your age. The number of credits you receive depends on how much you earn and when you earned it. You must earn a certain minimum amount for each quarter of credit, but you cannot be credited with more than 4 quarters in a year, regardless of how much money you make. Also called quarter or credit.

QMB

Qualified Medicare Beneficiary. For certain low-income elderly people who meet income and resource qualifications, state medical assistance (Medicaid) will pay the annual Medicare medical insurance premium, and may also pay the yearly Medicare medical insurance deductible and Medicare coinsurance. People eligible for this assistance are sometimes called "Quimbys."

RBRV

The Resource-Based Relative-Value scale establishes the rate Medicare will pay for each service a physician performs. The scale provides a formula based on the time, overhead, and liability insurance premiums of doctors applicable to each service or procedure.

Reasonable Fees and Charges

Medicare defines reasonable fees and charges as the lesser of:
- Your physician's or supplier's present or actual charge for a specific service.
- The customary fees the physician or supplier charges for a particular service.
- The prevailing charge for the service determined by the Medicare carrier under a procedure prescribed by Medi-

care law. The charges and fees deemed reasonable are generally not higher than the charges or fees of 3 out of 4 doctors or suppliers for the same services or supplies in the same area.

Recomputation

Refiguring your benefit is called a recomputation. It happens automatically if your reported wages cause the benefit to be decreased or increased, or you can request as recomputation from the SSA. If you disagree with the amount of benefit you have been assigned, or believe there is an error in your computation, you must make your request for a recomputation in writing. Be sure to include pertinent evidence with your letter, you will have to supply documents to substantiate your claim.

Reconsideration

If you are turned down for benefits (that is if you receive a "disallowance of benefits") you can request a review of your application. You must fill out a form at your Social Security office, and the form must be filed within 60 days of your receipt of the notice that your claim for benefits has been rejected.

Respite Care

Short-term care in a hospital to provide temporary relief to a person who regularly provides home care for a Medicare patient respite care is limited to 80 hours a year.

Retirement Test

See Earnings Limitation.

SECA

Self-Employed Contributions Act, or the Social Security taxes on income made by self-employed people. SECA taxes are paid entirely by the self-employed person and are currently equal to the percentage of wages paid by an employee and the employer combined.

Senior Corps

Part of the Corporation for National Service, the Senior Corps includes 760 local Retired Senior Volunteer programs (450,000 volunteers), the Foster Grandparent program (24,000 elders serving children with special needs), and the Senior Companions program (12,000 elders serving disabled elders). Service stipends paid by some of these programs are not counted when determining income or assets to qualify for SSI or disability.

Sequestration

This term is used in conjunction with the Gramm-Rudman-Hollings Act, which was passed, to force Congress to reduce and eventually eliminate the federal deficit by imposing across-the-board spending cuts. These cuts are made automatically if Congress fails to meet the October deadline for passing a budget that cuts spending enough to meet targeted reductions. Budgets for each government department are reduced (sequestered) by a certain percentage, and the longer Congress delays, the more the percentage increases.

Service Benefits

Service benefits are for people in or connected with the uniformed forces on active duty in the U.S. Army, Navy, Marines, Air Force, Coast Guard, and Coast and Geodetic Survey. Before 1957, uniformed services personnel did not pay Social Security taxes, but earned a credit of $160 for each month of active service. Since 1956, all service-connected personnel have paid Social Security taxes. Their credits are based on basic pay plus non-contributory wage credits of $100 for each $300 of wages received in a year up to $1,200 in any year.

SLMB

Specified Low-Income Medicare Beneficiary.

SMI

Supplementary Medical Insurance, another name for Medical Insurance, Medicare Part B.

SMI Trust Fund

Supplementary Medical Insurance trust fund. It generally receives premiums and matching payments made under the supplementary medical insurance program (Medicare Part B).

Social Security Integration

The law which allows a company to reduce a worker's pension by as much as 50% by deducting the amount the worker receives in Social Security benefits. See Permitted Disparity.

SSI

Supplemental Security Income.

Substantial Gainful Activity

The cap set on the amount of earnings allowable while collecting disability insurance. The amount of exempt earnings established by the SSA for an individual is generally considered substantial gainful work for the disabled or blind person receiving benefits.

Substantial Services

More than 45 hours of work per month in a trade or business. However, less than 45 hours per month may be considered substantial if it is spent in a highly skilled occupation, or in managing a sizable business.

Survivors' Benefits

Payments made to a living spouse (include some divorced spouses) or living children (in some cases, grandchildren or parents) of deceased worker who was covered by Social Security.

Terminal Illness

An illness expected to end in death.

Utilization Review

Traditional health insurance plans usually require a second opinion for surgery, nurse or doctor from the reviewing company will call your physician before approving hospital admissions (except emergencies). They also usually limit the number of days the plan will pay for care, or the amount the company will pay for the care.

The Utilization Review Committee of a hospital decides if a particular service is covered by Medicare or not. Sometimes the PRO or PSRO (Peer Review Organization or Professional Standards Review Organization) is the committee that does this review.

Veterans Benefits

The federal government has more than four different benefits and services for veterans of service in the armed forces. The payment procedures under all these programs are complex, particularly when benefits under the Social Security programs also come into play. The Veterans Administration has a publication explaining these benefits programs: Pamphlet 27-82-2 may be ordered from the VA Compensation Group, Office of Personnel Management, Washington, DC 20401. Fact Sheet IS-I, Federal Benefits for Veterans and Dependents, is available from the Government Printing Office, Washington DC 20402.

Voluntary Enrollment for Medical Insurance

Anyone age 65 or over and not eligible for Medicare hospital insurance (Part A) under Social Security may buy the coverage. For 1996, the basic premium for voluntarily enrollment for Medicare Part A is $289 per month. But if you want to buy hospital insurance, you have to enroll for Part B medical insurance and pay that monthly premium as well. The Part B premium for 1996 is $42.50 per month. Time restrictions for signing up are the same as for those eligible under Social Security coverage. See Enrollment Periods.

Wage Indexing

An adjustment procedure by which the earnings record of a worker is related to the national average earnings in the indexing year. The indexing year is the second year before the year in which the worker becomes 62, is disabled, or dies. For example, if a worker becomes 62 in 1996, the indexing year is 1994.

Windfall

Refers to unexpected outcomes of legislative measures or regulations that result in some people receiving much larger benefit amounts than intended.

Work Record

The record kept by the SSA of the wages you have in covered employment and the Social Security taxes you have paid over the years you have worked. The SSA sometimes refers to this record as your "account." Your work record determines your eligibility for benefits and the amount of benefits to which you are entitled, so it pays to be sure it is accurate. Check by requesting a Personal Earnings and Benefit Estimate Statement from the SSA.

Spinal-Cord Injuries

Thousands of Americans receive injuries to their spinal cords or to their brain in car crashes, sports accidents or even in their own homes.

For many years scientists have been puzzled by the mystery of why connections in the central nervous system, the brain and spinal cord do not repair themselves while connections in the peripheral nervous system can.

A team led by Martin Schwab of the Brain Research Institute at the University of Zurich in Switzerland have been working for more than 15 years on the identification of a gene that prevents nerve-cell connections in the central nervous system from regenerating after they are cut or damaged.

The team has now identified a gene that produces a protein that prevents such nerve-cell regeneration. They call it the NOGO gene because of its inhibiting effect on regeneration.

Their experiments on rats have disclosed that when the protein is blocked the spinal cord can repair itself. Findings of the Swiss Team were reported in the journal *Nature* by scientists in Switzerland, England and the United States.

The Schwab team has reported the discovery of an antibody that blocks the NOGO-created protein. In test tube experiments nerves dissected from laboratory rats were exposed to the antibody. The nerves regrew hundreds of nerve connections known as axons, or tiny branches that transmit impulses from one nerve cell to the next. In other experiments that were not reported in *Nature* the team said that it cut the spinal cords of rats, paralyzing the animals and then gave the animals the antibody for two weeks.

The nerves grew and the animals resumed normal activities such as grabbing food pellets and climbing a rope.

Neurologists laud the work as a landmark but caution that other factors may also inhibit regrowth. Dr. Ben Barres of the neurology department of Stanford University stated "It is important not to give patients false hope but I think there are a lot of grounds for optimism now." Solomon Snyder a top neurologist at Johns Hopkins University who was not involved in the research states "It looks very promising that NOGO is a key factor that explains why nerves do not regenerate in the brain. The road to developing nerve therapies based on this straight forward." Smith-Kline Beecham, Philadelphia, and other groups are working to identify a molecular receptor in the brain for NOGO.

Christopher Reeve who was paralyzed in a riding accident and his foundation have helped in some of the NOGO research at Yale University. It was reported that Mr. Reeves hopes to take part in human tests by the Schwab team in about 5 years.

This information has been included in this work to assist readers in keeping up with the current status of events and discoveries in this area.

Health Care Documents

This appendix contains three different sample documents; a Durable Power of Attorney for Health Care, a Living Will, and a Specific Statement of Health Care Wishes.

These sample documents will help you get an idea of the arrangements you can make to insure that your wishes about your medical treatment, should you not be able to make them known at the time will be carried out.

If you are interested in making such arrangements, these samples offer a range of options to help you decide what document or documents would best suit your needs. A lawyer who knows your state's latest legal requirements will then be able to prepare the papers for you. You should also discuss your health options with your physician, and the person or persons you name to act for you, as well as your attorney.

We suggest you review your healthcare documents periodically, and that you keep them where they can be easily found.

Durable Power of Attorney for Health Care

If and when you sign a Durable Power of Attorney for Health Care (also called a healthcare proxy), you are the "grantor" and grant to someone else to communicate those wishes yourself. A Durable Power of Attorney goes into effect immediately after it is signed, though the grantor still makes those decisions until it is needed. It remains valid for the life of the person assigning it, but can be revoked at any time.

TO WHOM IT MAY CONCERN

I, _____ Social Security # _____

residing at _____

do hereby appoint _____

residing at _____

as my ATTORNEY-IN-FACT, hereafter to by such title, to make health and personal care decisions and to exercise such other powers for me as authorized herein. My ATTORNEY-IN-FACT shall use the following form when signing on my behalf pursuant to this Power:

_____ by _____ ATTORNEY-IN-FACT.
(Name of GRANTOR)   (Name)

I intend to create a DURABLE POWER OF ATTORNEY FOR HEALTH pursuant to Section ___ of the Status of the State of _____ and hereby revoke any prior Powers of Attorney for Health heretofore executed by me.

I grant to my ATTORNEY-IN-FACT the following powers, such powers to be used for my benefit and on my behalf and to be exercised only in a fiduciary capacity and to be effective upon and only during any period of incapacity in which, in the opinion of my ATTORNEY-IN-FACT and attending physician, I am unable to make or communicate a choice regarding any healthcare decision:

1. To arrange for my entrance to and care at any hospital, nursing home, health center, convalescent home, retirement home, or similar institution, and to authorize, arrange for, consent to, waive and terminate any and all medical and surgical procedures on my behalf, including but not limited to the use of mechanical or other procedures that affect bodily function, artificial respiration, nutritional support and hydration, cardiopulmonary resuscitation and administration of drugs.

2. To hire and discharge any medical, home care services or other personnel responsible for my healthcare.

3. To recommend or refuse to recommend or authorize any medication to relieve pain or other condition notwithstanding the fact that such decision may lead to addiction or other damage or shorten the remaining period of my life.

4. To contract for any medical or other healthcare service or facility on my behalf without personal liability of any kind by my ATTORNEY-IN-FACT for the same.

5. To execute on my behalf any waivers or releases of liability required by any Hospital, Physician, or other provider of Health Care, any authorizations relating to the refusal of treatment, or discharge from a Hospital or other Institution contrary to medical advice that such conduct would endanger my life or my physical condition.

6. To undertake any legal action that may be necessary to enforce my wishes or directives herein under my name and at my expense or at the expense of my estate.

7. To obtain and have access to my medical records and information contained therein in the same manner as I might have been able to do without limitation.

8. To follow any healthcare provisions that I may have made in any Living Will duly executed by me.

9. If I have a condition that is incurable or irreversible and without the use of life sustaining procedures will result in death within a relatively short time, I now declare that I do not want the application of such life-sustaining procedures administered. This directive shall also apply if I am in a coma or vegetative state which is reasonably concluded by my physician and ATTORNEY-IN-FACT to be irreversible.

10. In making the decisions herein by my ATTORNEY-IN-FACT I want my ATTORNEY-IN-FACT to weigh the relief of my suffering, the expense and the quality of my life and the effect of any extension of my life in making such decisions and in the event of any conflict of opinion as to whether or not such decisions are appropriate or legal the opinion of my ATTORNEY-IN-FACT shall be final and conclusive without the coccurrence of any other person or authority.

In the event that my ATTORNEY-IN-FACT shall be unable or unwilling to exercise the powers herein granted, or be deceased, or if the ATTORNEY-IN-FACT is my spouse and is legally separated or divorced from me, then in such event I do hereby appoint _____ as SUCCESSOR ATTORNEY-IN-FACT, to act in such capacity.

Any person who acts in good faith upon the representations of my ATTORNEY-IN-FACT, or designated SUCCESSOR herein, shall not be liable to me, to my estate, my heirs or personal representatives, for such or actions taken by them.

This DURABLE POWER OF ATTORNEY shall be valid in any jurisdiction in which the powers are exercised or presented as the authority for any action stated herein. In the event that any power herein granted is declared invalid by any Court such invalidity shall not invalidate this instrument or any other powers herein granted.

IN WITNESS WHEREOF, I have hereunto affixed my hand and seal this day _____, 19 ___.

_____
(Legal signature)

Specific Statement of Health Care Wishes

If there are certain types of treatments or procedures that you do or do not want, you may wish to have a document like the following one as well as the general statement to the physician.

It is very important, given the nature of these sorts of statements, that you discuss this statement with your physician, who can give you any medical information you may need. You also must make the existence of such a document known and make it part of your medical records.

CONDITIONS
Initial the blanks to correspond with your wishes.

__ If I am in a persistent vegetative state, or coma, and in the opinion of my physician(s) have little or no known hope of surviving or regaining awareness and higher mental functions, no matter what is done.

__ If I have brain damage, or some brain disease, that cannot be reversed, which makes me unable to recognize people or to speak understandably, but have no terminal illness and can live in this condition for a long time.

__ If I have a terminal illness, such as incurable cancer, which will be a likely cause of my death.

TREATMENT AND PROCEDURES

1. Cardiopulmonary resuscitation: the use (on patients who are at the point of dying) of drugs, chest compression, or electric shock to start the heart beating; artificial breathing

      want   do not want   undecided   trial; stop if no improvement

2. Mechanical ventilation: breathing by machine

      want   do not want   undecided   trial; stop if no improvement

3. Artificial nutrition and hydration: nutrition and fluid given through a tube in the veins, nose to stomach

      want   do not want   undecided   trial; stop if no improvement

4. Major Surgery: such as removing the gallbladder or part of the intestines

      want   do not want   undecided

5. Kidney Dialysis: cleaning the blood by machine or by fluid passed through the belly

      want   do not want   undecided   trial; stop if no improvement

6. Chemotherapy: the use of drugs to fight cancer

      want   do not want   undecided   trial; stop if no improvement

7. Major Surgery:

_____   _____   _____
    want   do not want   undecided

8. Invasive diagnostic tests: such as using a flexible tube to look into the stomach

_____   _____   _____   _____
    want   do not want   undecided   trial; stop if no improvement

9. Blood or blood products:

_____   _____   _____   _____
    want   do not want   undecided   trial; stop if no improvement

10. Antibiotics: drugs to fight infection

_____   _____   _____   _____
    want   do not want   undecided   trial; stop if no improvement

11. Simple diagnostic tests: such as blood tests or x-rays

_____   _____   _____   _____
    want   do not want   undecided   trial; stop if no improvement

12. Pain medications: even if they dull consciousness and indirectly shorten life

_____   _____   _____   _____
    want   do not want   undecided   trial; stop if no improvement

13. Other treatments: You may also list other specific treatments you DO NOT WANT, such as treatment in an intensive care unit. I especially do not want:

_____

_____

_____

You may add instruction for other care YOU WANT, such as pain medication or your preference to die at home if possible. Other instructions:

_____

_____

_____

Signed: _____   Dated: _____

_____

Living Will

The following document is a general statement of healthcare wishes, usually called a living will, to direct your physician when you are no longer able to speak for yourself.

If you decide to execute a living will, be sure to discuss it with your attorney and physician. Have you attorney prepare the living will and supervise its execution by you in the presence of witnesses to conform to requirements of your state's laws. You should then have a copy included in your medical records.

I, wish to participate in my own medical care as long as I am able. But recognizing that an accident or illness may someday make me unable to do so, this document is intended to direct those who make choices on my behalf. I have prepared it while still legally competent and of sound mind. If these instructions create a conflict with desires of my relatives, or with hospital policies, or with the principles of those providing my care, I ask that my instructions prevail. I wish to live a full and long life, but not at all costs. If my death is near and cannot be avoided, and I have lost the ability to interact with others and have no reasonable chance of regaining this ability, or if my suffering is intense and irreversible, I do not want to have my life prolonged. I would then ask not to be subjected to life-prolonging procedures, other than any treatments or procedures that I have initialed in a Specific Statement of My Wishes. I would wish, rather, to have only the sort of care which gives comfort and support, which facilitates my interaction with others to the extent possible, and which brings peace.

Signed: _____   Witnesses: _____

Date: _____   _____

SOCIAL SECURITY ADMINISTRATION
WILKES-BARRE DATA OPERATIONS CENTER
P.O. BOX 7004
WILKES-BARRE, PA 18767-7004

Request for Earnings and Benefit Estimate Statement

Please print or type your answers. When you have completed the form, fold it and mail it to us.

1. Name shown on your Social Security card:

_____
First   Last   Initial

2. Your Social Security number as shown on your card:

☐☐☐ - ☐☐ - ☐☐☐☐

3. Your date of birth _____ _____ _____
                      Month   Day   Year

4. Other Social Security numbers you have used:

☐☐☐ - ☐☐ - ☐☐☐☐

☐☐☐ - ☐☐ - ☐☐☐☐

5. Your sex: ☐ Male ☐ Female

6. Other names you have used:
   (including a maiden name):

_____

_____

For items 7 and 9 show only earnings covered by Social Security. Do NOT include wages from State, local or Federal Government employment that are NOT covered for Social Security or that are covered ONLY by Medicare.

7. Show your actual earnings (wages and/or net self-employment income for last year)

   A. Last year's actual earnings: *(Dollars Only)*

      $ ☐☐☐ , ☐☐☐ . ☐☐

   B. This year's estimated earnings: *(Dollars Only)*

      $ ☐☐☐ , ☐☐☐ . ☐☐

8. Show the age at which you plan to stop working.

   ☐☐
   (Show only one age)

9. Below, show the average yearly amount (not your total future lifetime earnings that you think you will earn between now and when you plan to stop working. Include cost-of-living, performance or scheduled pay increases or bonuses.

   If you expect to earn significantly more or less in the future due to promotions, job changes, partime work, or an absence from the work force, enter the amount that closely reflects your future average yearly earnings.

   If you don't expect any significant changes, show the same amount you are earning now (the amount in 7B).

   Future average yearly earnings: *(Dollars Only)*

   $ ☐☐☐ , ☐☐☐ . ☐☐

10. Address where you want us to send the statement.

Name _____

City _____ State ____ Zip Code ____

11. ☐ Please check this box if you want to get your statement in Spanish instead of English.

Notice:

I am asking for the information about my own Social Security record or the record of a person I am authorized to represent. I understand that if I deliberately request information under false pretenses I may be guilty of a federal crime and could be fined and/or imprisoned. I authorize you to use a contractor to send the statement of earnings and benefit estimates to the person named in item 10.

Please sign your name (Do not print)

▲
_____
Signature

_____
Date   (Area Code) Daytime Telephone No.